EARTH
ACUPUNCTURE

"An eminently readable compilation of both Eastern and Western geomantic techniques . . . *Earth Acupuncture* is an excellent book . . ."

SIG LONEGREN, GEOMANCER AND
AUTHOR OF *SACRED SPACE HANDBOOK*

EARTH ACUPUNCTURE

Healing the Living Landscape

GAIL REICHSTEIN REX, L.Ac.

Bear & Company
Rochester, Vermont • Toronto, Canada

Bear & Company
One Park Street
Rochester, Vermont 05767
www.BearandCompanyBooks.com

Text stock is certified

Bear & Company is a division of Inner Traditions International

Figures 2.1, 2.3, 2.4, 3.1, 3.2, 4.1, 4.2, and 6.2 originally published in *The Web That Has No Weaver* by Ted Kaptchuk and used by permission of the author.

Library of Congress Cataloging-in-Publication Data
Names: Reichstein, Gail.
Title: Earth acupuncture : healing the living landscape / Gail Reichstein Rex.
Description: Rochester, Vermont : Bear & Company, 2016. | Includes
  bibliographical references and index.
Identifiers: LCCN 2015029861| ISBN 9781591432029 (pbk.) |
ISBN 9781591437819 (e-book)
Subjects: LCSH: Landscape protection. | Nature conservation. | Environmental
  health. | Reclamation of land.
Classification: LCC QH75 .R4356 2016 | DDC 333.73—dc23
LC record available at http://lccn.loc.gov/2015029861

Printed and bound in the United States by Lake Book Manufacturing, Inc. The text stock is SFI certified. The Sustainable Forestry Initiative® program promotes sustainable forest management.

10 9 8 7 6 5 4 3 2 1

Text design and layout by Debbie Glogover
This book was typeset in Garamond Premier Pro with Optima LT Std, Gill Sans
  MT Pro, and Adobe Wood Type Ornament for display fonts

To send correspondence to the author of this book, mail a first-class letter to the author c/o Inner Traditions • Bear & Company, One Park Street, Rochester, VT 05767, and we will forward the communication.

Contents

Foreword

For hundreds of thousands of years, traditional cultures have managed to live in long-term sustainable relationship with their landscapes. Yet what was once second nature now seems nearly out of reach: our global, mechanized culture is so entrenched that we may rightly question whether it is even possible to get there—back to a seamless relationship and balance—from here.

It seems to me that it is entirely possible and that we have in fact lost only two key things on our long journey from there to here: a sense that time is cyclical, and an awareness of the sentient intelligence of the natural world. When we look at sustainable cultures, we see that these two elements are present in their understanding of the world. Perhaps if we could reinstate these two elements in our own culture, they would allow us the harmonious long-range future that we all desire.

First, a sustainable paradigm includes an awareness of time as having a circular nature—of wax and wane, of seasons passing, but always returning around and around the wheel of life, of circumstance, and of opportunity.

We presently have a linear view of time as something that stretches out from us to an unknown and unseen future of possibilities of increase and more of everything. This unseen future creates a need for our economies to grow rather than to sustain. Unfortunately, that which grows forever unchecked without the balance of reduction is a cancer in biological terms: our linear concept of time is thus introducing a cancerous consciousness into our dealings with each other and our environment. In contrast, circular time awareness brings us back to living in a renewable relationship in so many parts of our life and activities.

The second great key is an awareness of the sentient intelligence surrounding us—the many and various intelligences of nature, including our elemental environment. Collectively, these intelligences combine to create a spirit of place. Our awareness of the spirited sentience around us then becomes the basis of communication with our natural environment, allowing it to support our endeavors and guide our minds cooperatively and cocreatively.

Across the planet and throughout the ages, there has been a deep reverence for, and a cultivated relationship with, the spirit of place. For much of human history, nature has been regarded as sentient and the body of the planet has been understood as a living being—much like the body of a person, with meridians of energy flowing both above- and belowground. These pathways of flowing energy, composed of electricity, magnetism, life force, and chi, form the energetic anatomy of the Earth's subtle body.

Below our feet, geomagnetism follows the conductive pathways of underground water, geological faults and fissures, and seams of crystals and minerals. These pathways are known to geophysics as telluric currents.

Above us, there are condensations and harmonic standing waves in the atmosphere—the so-called Schuman resonances—that create a spider's web of electromagnetic connectivity above ground. Perceived directly by human sensitivity and observed by their effects on plants and animals and the health of individuals and communities, these pathways of flowing life energy are the dragons known in east and west, north and south.

Song lines, spirit paths, leys, routes of ancient pilgrimage: they go by many names across cultures and history but are universally regarded. These meridians are traditionally energized by human attention and activated to connect sacred sites and pathways.

Both ancient wisdom and contemporary practice show that when the manifold energies of a place are in harmonious balance, agricultural fertility is greatly enhanced. In my own work with farmers around the world, I have found that germination rates increase up to fourfold and crop yields increase between 20 and 300 percent.

Conversely, when the Earth's meridians are discordant, stressed, or sluggish—a condition known as *geopathic stress*—human health is adversely affected. Earth acupuncture is an ancient and powerful way of harmonizing geopathic stress and connecting human consciousness with the spirit of place. It is known to have been practiced in ancient Egypt, and the "needles of stone" of the Neolithic and Bronze Ages are still in evidence in Europe and the British Isles. Temple pinnacles and church spires can also be accurately understood as earth needles, balancing the energies between heaven and earth to increase landscape fertility and human, plant, and animal health.

There is a great resurgence of awareness and interest in this area, traditionally known as *geomancy,* with many strands of knowledge coming together, from Eastern and Western traditions, and from ancient knowledge and contemporary experimentation.

In this beautifully written book, Gail Rex generously shares her own journey of discovery, increasing awareness, and healing intervention on one of North America's primary meridians. Her account and description of her perceptions and understandings are an inspiration to all of us seeking closer connection with our living environment and offer pathways that we can follow in our own fashion to help restore the natural balance and harmony around us that we and all species may thrive and flourish.

I urge the reader to engage with her story with an open heart, an inquiring mind, an active imagination—and once engaged and inspired, to try it out at home. . . .

PATRICK MACMANAWAY, MBCHB

Dr. Patrick MacManaway is a second-generation, international practitioner of the healing arts and of geomancy and earth acupuncture. Past president of the British Society of Dowsers, he holds a degree in medicine from Edinburgh University, is cofounder and design consultant for Circles for Peace, and is the author of several books and CDs.

Acknowledgments

I am grateful to the many beings who shared their wisdom and experience with me during the time these events took place—all of those who are mentioned in this book as well as the legions who are not. I hope that the telling of our co-created story will bring benefit to all.

Thanks, also, to Jon Graham, Laura Schlivek, and everyone at Inner Traditions who helped in the creation of this book. With the tale now in print, my commitment to the river feels fulfilled.

And I am grateful beyond words to Robert, my husband, whose early and unfailing support for me in the telling of this story made it all possible. His enthusiasm and love are tremendous blessings in my life.

And to Orion, seed of the new future, who is already a friend to Moheakantuk.

Wadogh.

Healing the Earth with Natural Medicine

Since my first day of acupuncture school nearly twenty-five years ago, I have been fascinated by the way that Chinese medicine connects human health with the patterns and cycles of nature. Early in my practice I wrote a book about the five-element cycle and the precise ways it defines how each of us mirrors the world around us. "The planet and its creatures are made of the same stuff," I wrote in *Wood Becomes Water*. "We suffer from the same illnesses and will heal from the same cures. We are *that* closely intertwined."*

At the time, I meant that we can find ways of healing our bodies by learning from natural cycles. Little did I know that just a few years later I'd be turning that model on its head, using acupuncture and the principles of Chinese medicine to heal a river near my home. This time, instead of looking to nature for insights into healing the human body, I was applying the techniques of human medicine to illnesses of the natural world. Healing from the same cures indeed.

Acupuncture for the earth. It is not exactly a new idea but is not widely practiced either. That our rivers and valleys and forests might

---

*Gail Reichstein, *Wood Becomes Water: Chinese Medicine in Everyday Life* (New York: Kodansha, 1998).

be capable of illness and of healing—just like a person—suggests a landscape more animated than we commonly allow. Yet natural medicine for the planet is on the cusp of a resurgence, in part because it provides a rare hopeful response to the plague of global destruction. Like natural medicine for people, medicine for the planet fills a deep collective need by opening us to a model of healing that is more compassionate, more empowering, and often more effective than standard practice.

Modern medicine is focused so exclusively on illness that it is often frustrating for doctors and patients alike. A system that sees only what needs to be killed off, removed, reduced, or replaced cannot help but leave us wanting, for it fails to make use of what is best in us—our fragments of good health, our inner strength, and our capacities for love and growth. Yet these are the exact resources that engender true healing.

One of the greatest contributions that acupuncture and other natural medicines make to our modern life is the concept of healing as a process of growth. More than just an absence of disease, healing is an ongoing activity that we can engage ourselves in every day. We can become more well even as certain parts of us are struggling. We can be healing even if we are manifestly ill.

In this model, we heal through the integration of forces around and within us. New ideas or experiences that stabilize the body and mind increase our capacity to organize ourselves, allowing us to integrate more elements into our smooth functioning. Integrating more means being disrupted by less, so we have less dissonance in our lives, less chaos, less illness—more positive growth.

In the course of the adventure that fills these pages, I realized that our planet needs natural medicine, too. Just reducing the many pollutions we have created—even if it were possible and achieved within our lifetimes—is not going to make our Earth well. The landscape needs healing: it needs help integrating and organizing the multitudinous influences we humans have brought to it.

● ● ●

When acupuncturists work with clients we spend a lot of time looking and listening, asking and touching; these are the four principles that guide every session and direct our diagnosis and treatment. They ensure that we create a relationship with each client, every time: a relationship based on two-way communication—asking and listening, giving and receiving.

To my great surprise, I have discovered that healing work with nature depends on these same elements exactly: asking and listening, giving and receiving. Although the specifics of the interactions are different and don't involve language, the experience of relating to a tree or a mountain is as genuine as relating to anything else that doesn't talk: an infant, a loved one asleep, a horse, a cat. It is our openness that defines how clearly we can perceive their needs, and our creativity and generosity that determine how completely we can meet those needs. When we accept that our planet embodies a level of complexity that is beyond our comprehension, just like our loved ones, we take the first steps toward the mutual respect that is the foundation of every relationship and of every healing.

There are many ways to promote the regeneration of the Earth. I have met dowsers, shamans, priestesses, meditators, feng shui masters, and activists of all kinds who regularly apply themselves to healing on a grand scale. Many people from all walks of life are already dedicated to fostering positive growth in the people around them. It takes only a leap of faith to begin applying the same compassion and skills to plants, animals, and landscapes.

The story that follows is the tale of my effort to bring healing to a particular landscape—the stretch of the Hudson River that abuts the Indian Point Nuclear Power Plant in Buchanan, New York. It happens that I worked largely within the language and structures of Chinese medicine, but that is just incidental. You can find healing in any language, or with no language at all; mute wonder is also an effective agent of healing.

PART I

Diagnosis

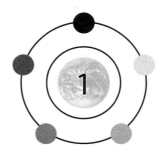

The Dragon's Breath

In October of 2002, I had a vision. I was sitting in a meditation class when I began to see clear images in my mind.

From a bird's-eye view, I saw the Hudson River—the section near Peekskill, New York, where three big curves mark a zigzag passage at the southern end of the Hudson Highlands. Like a movie projected on a screen in my head, I saw sparks from the Indian Point nuclear power plant, which sits on the eastern shore of the river on a spit of land that was once an amusement park, and long before that a gathering place for the area's indigenous people. The sparks looked like lightning bolts arcing continuously from the plant into the river. They also seeped into the ground and stretched lavalike tongues of fire into the riverbed in all directions. My vision zoomed in, focusing on these crackling fires that pulsed through the riverbed, and I felt a whirl of sensations: a kind of nausea, a choking feeling, and something like disbelief. The power plant was leaking poison into the earth, and the river was showing me its injuries. This display made my heart ache, and then the images began to fade. A voice spoke in my head saying, "What you are given to see, you can heal. Work with the hills."

My attention came back to the room I was sitting in. I was stunned and fought to concentrate on what was going on around me. "Work with the hills," the voice had said. What could that even mean?

In deep meditation odd things happen sometimes: you have sudden insights, develop new understanding, give birth to ideas. When something emerges out of stillness like that it's a powerful and humbling experience, so I try to pay attention. But I'd never before had pictures come to me out of the blue, unrelated to anything I'd been thinking about. And I'd certainly never heard a voice. I did briefly wonder if I was crazy—seeing things and hearing voices that weren't there. I didn't feel delusional, but that wasn't particularly reassuring. At least the voice was instructing me to heal—that fact did calm me down a little. Still, I promised myself that I'd be on watch for any more weird behavior; I did not want to be losing touch with reality.

During the rest of that weekend's seminar I felt quite normal. I enjoyed the meditations, had a nice time getting to know the other participants, and felt like I was getting a lot out of the class. Driving home from Vermont to New York on Sunday, I cautiously allowed myself to think about the vision again. It had been an intense experience. What should I do about it? I could ignore it, but found I didn't want to. If I had received a spiritual message from the Hudson River, I wanted to acknowledge it. Though I had been driving for hours and was eager to get home, I decided to continue an extra few minutes in order to stand by the Hudson before the sun went down. I didn't have any plan in mind, but I knew I wanted to see the river.

I drove to the tiny beach at Little Stony Point. It was late afternoon, crisp October, and an autumn-red sunset scattered its light on the water. I moved in close to the water's edge and saw the dark-green river splashing against the rocks. The primitive, algal smell and the rhythmic lap of the water were comforting, and I decided I could stop worrying about losing my mind. If I was having a breakdown, I'd know it soon enough. In the meantime, why not embrace this new experience?

I took a good look at the water all around. It didn't look hurt, but how would I be able to tell? It didn't look exactly at ease, either. I spoke to the river from my mind. "River, are you in pain?" I replayed the vision I had seen of the nuclear power plant, trying to "send" the images somehow to the spirit of the river. I made an effort to imagine what the river felt, having nuclear fission on its banks: splitting atoms and their decaying isotopes; heat and fire churning out electricity in the place where cool, wet darkness had reigned for millennia. The ecosystem was unaccustomed to these new forces; how chaotic it all must feel! I sprinkled a bit of cornmeal and sage into the river—traditional Native offerings as I'd been taught to make them—and I made a promise: that I would do whatever I was supposed to do to help the river heal. Without the faintest idea of what that would be, I simply vowed to be open to finding out.

After I made a promise to the river, I wondered what would come of it. Going through the daily motions of work and rest, I felt a bit fragile— anxious that some lightning bolt of obligation might strike and change everything, and at the same time, worried that the next message would be so subtle that I would miss it altogether. I didn't know how I was going to make good on my vow, but I knew I didn't want to bumble around with random projects that *might* be healing for the river, just to feel that I was doing something; I wanted my steps to be as guided and sure as the vision. I decided to cultivate stillness, inside and out, in order to make space for new insights, but where would the guidance come from?

For better or for worse, stillness was not a difficult environment to cultivate. My life was very quiet. I was single, unattached, and living in an unincorporated village within a small town. I rented a house on a dirt road in the middle of the woods. It had been built in the early 1800s on a quiet lane that later became part of a fourteen-thousand-acre state park. I had two neighbors within shouting distance, but that was about it for a mile or more in every direction.

My friends were mostly couples—some with kids—who didn't have much time for socializing, so I spent a lot of time by myself. When I wasn't seeing clients for acupuncture, I was usually reading, walking in the woods around my house, or working on art and writing projects at home. The meditation practice I had stumbled across the year before had been exciting because it felt like a powerful way to channel all my quietude into something constructive. Meditation turned my loneliness into strength.

Now I had something new to focus on. I spent time looking at books about the Hudson River, reading articles about Indian Point, gazing again and again at the magnificent points of scenery that the river and its banks afforded. I discovered that the Hudson is a 315-mile estuary of the Atlantic Ocean. This means that tides from the ocean at the river's basin push into the river itself, making it salty and marshy for over 120 miles. The tides also change the river's current, so that twice a day the river runs south to north as the tide rolls in, then runs north to south when the tide goes out. In fact, the Algonquin Indians who settled in the region some forty thousand years ago called the river *Moheakantuk*—"The Water That Is Never Still" or "The River That Runs Two Ways." The Mohican tribe, whose traditional territory included the river and surrounding valley, are named for this water.

For thousands of years, Moheakantuk and the lands around it provided the area's native people with a rich and abundant life. Offering plenty of fish and game, a variety of trees and soils, furs and woods for shelter and protection, the valley supported dozens of related clans and tribes. Over time, the native populations of the river highlands diversified into a network of woodland tribes including the Wappingers, Delawares, and Mohicans, who all lived and traded in the area between Manhattan and the Mohawk River junction, where the Iroquois Confederacy territory began.

These were the people that Henry Hudson met when he sailed his schooner the *Half Moon* up the river in 1609. Traveling as far as what we now call Albany, Hudson remarked that the land was "as pleasant with grass and flowers and goodly trees as ever they had seen."[1]

Other Dutch travelers began to settle in the region, drawn by the praise of Hudson and his crew. The new settlers, too, enjoyed the land of plenty—finding game, fish, woodlands, and ready transport along the river to the growing population center of Manhattan. The Dutch called the river by the man who had first sailed it: Henry Hudson.

The period of colonization that began in the years after Hudson's journey brought rapid change to the landscape and to its original inhabitants. As adventure seekers and opportunists from many places flocked to New Amsterdam/New York to take advantage of its abundant natural resources, they filled the countryside with forts and towns and traffic. The "melting pot" of America began here among polyglot settlers who eagerly fought, traded, and swindled—primarily from the natives but also among themselves—to gain a foothold.

The long and rich history of the river came as a surprise to me. Perhaps I had known some of it at an earlier point in my life, but whatever scattered details I had learned in high school had long since disappeared from mind. Reading this history now as a pageant of early America, I found it to be a dramatic and focused story. For most of its coexistence with humans, the Hudson River had been a centerpiece of life—a mainstay of food, resources, transportation, recreation, and defense for thousands of years. But the past two hundred years had changed all of that. The factories, foundries, and power plants located on the Hudson had, since their inception, appreciated the river mainly for the convenience it provided those industries: a ready source of water, a convenient way to dispose of pollution, and transportation to major markets. No longer valued for its living and life-giving attributes, Moheakantuk became merely a conduit for products and waste. Now this diminished and disrespected river was calling for help.

In November, I went back to Vermont to attend a workshop on the Native American medicine wheel—a version of the circle of life that appears in many cultures around the world as labyrinths, mandalas, zodiacs, and henges. In the class, we explored the ways that a medicine wheel—or any such mandala—is an inherently stabilizing force. By organizing thoughts, actions, and energies into specific patterns, these mandalas can precipitate strength out of chaos.

I had long been interested in henges and stone circles, especially the kinds that align themselves with particular days of the year, like equinoxes and solstices. I'd even been dreaming of building a stone circle somewhere near my home. The idea that such a structure could benefit the land it stood upon was new to me, but immediately exciting. In my acupuncture practice I use needles to stabilize people's health every day—why wouldn't stones placed thoughtfully in the ground do the same thing for the landscape?

I wondered if I could build a stone circle to help heal the Hudson River. The thought was electrifying. Suddenly, the acupuncturist, the mystic, the stone circle enthusiast, the environmentalist, and the natural healer in me all made sense together and made me feel that I had exactly the skills such a project would require. I didn't have any idea how I would actually accomplish it, but I decided in that minute that this would be the manifestation of my vow to the Hudson: a stone circle to help heal the landscape.

Unsure how to begin a project that seemed so big, I decided to ask the teacher of the workshop for advice. Venerable Dhyani Ywahoo is a twenty-seventh-generation teacher of the practices of the Cherokee people. Knowing that she was raised in a culture that recognizes the Earth and all creatures on it as sentient, sacred beings, I hoped that Venerable Dhyani might have some interesting ideas about healing a river.

During a question-and-answer period that afternoon, I announced that I was thinking of building a stone circle to help heal the land around the Indian Point nuclear power plant. I was nervous saying it out loud in case people in the class thought the idea was silly, or too complicated, or grandiose. My heart thumped, and I could hear my voice quavering as I spoke. To my great wonder, Venerable Dhyani responded as though I'd said the most normal thing in the world.

"Some people hear the cries of the land," she said quite matter-of-factly. "It is good to apply your skills of healing in answer to those cries." And just like that, my idea began to seem achievable.

"You can take the pulse of the Earth just like you do with a person,"

Venerable Dhyani continued. This was a surprise; I hadn't expected suggestions on how to do it. "The scale is a little bit different, so instead of your three fingers on a person's wrist, you would take pulses at three miles, six miles, and nine miles away from the power plant. You also want to find the place where the dragon exhales its bad breath, and there is where you will build your circle."

Hmm. Like a mystic riddle or an old-time prophecy, these directions were almost incomprehensible, yet deeply poetic. The "dragon's bad breath"? The "pulse of the Earth"? How would I begin to find such things? Still, as odd as they sounded, Venerable Dhyani's words at least gave me a place to begin. Mulling over her suggestions as I made the five-hour drive back home the next day, I stopped at a convenience store to buy a map of the Hudson Highlands region. My hands were trembling as I paid for the map; I was nervous and excited to be taking this first step.

The next day I spread the map of northern Westchester County onto my large dining table and stared at the river for a while. I realized I'd never seen the Indian Point power plant up close. Though I drove by it several times a week on the way to and from my office, it was a mile from the main road and surrounded by massive industrial buildings. There is a public park that abuts the power station's land, but the plant itself is invisible from that vantage point. Closer in, gated (and guarded) access roads keep trespassers out.

I wanted to get a good view of the monster I was dealing with and decided the best way to do this would be to cross to the western bank of the river and look back at Indian Point from there. On the map I could see that a large swath of parkland covered the area directly across the river from Indian Point; I made that my destination and went exploring.

Driving across the Bear Mountain Bridge, I was impressed again with the beauty of the region. The views of the meandering river and the low mountains alongside it are breathtaking and provocative. "World-class scenery," says my friend Teresa. "Less dramatic than the Alps or the San Francisco Bay, perhaps, but just as stunning in its own way." She is right. Grand but not overwhelming, the Hudson Highlands are a wild majesty.

During the Revolutionary War, the Highlands were viewed by both sides as vital to control of the region. They became a central battleground, as well as a symbol of Revolutionary power and an important part of George Washington's command. After independence, early Americans took pride in the Hudson's role in the birth of the nation; with the advent of steamboat travel, they began to travel on the river to better appreciate its history.

The astounding scenery that accompanied the Revolution's history made the Hudson Highlands a valued tourist destination, particularly among cultured Europeans who came to taste the air of the new country. It was in this period that the painters Thomas Cole, Asher Durand, and others created a new American tradition—the Hudson River School—in their efforts to capture the beauty and wildness of the river on canvas. The Hudson River School painters who celebrated this landscape, and the writers who worked alongside them, read into the land a story of power: the settlers who subdued the wilderness were at once heroes and ordinary men—the avatars of American exceptionalism. Though the land on both sides of the river is now largely tamed and suburbanized, this stretch of the Highlands maintains a rugged beauty.

During the mid-nineteenth century, the Hudson provided popular outings for day-trippers, with steamboats setting off from Manhattan multiple times a day to bring weary New Yorkers to the cool and refreshing mountains. After the Civil War and the Great Westward Expansion of the mid-1800s, however, the country's romantic imagination began to turn away from the hilly, wooded caverns of the Hudson and toward the wide-open expanses of the West. The Hudson began to fade as a visual symbol of scenic America and became instead an active center of industry and transportation; the Erie Canal helped turn the Hudson into a major commercial throughway to the West, and the railroad eased transportation to points north and south.

In time, steamboat landings and amusement parks were replaced by shipyards, dye works, brick works, tanneries, and iron forges that hummed and clanged along the riverside, all of them turning their effluent over to the river in lieu of managed disposal. When Consolidated Edison bought Indian Point and began to build its nuclear power station there in the 1950s, it was welcomed as a tax-paying replacement for the tourist traffic that had all but disappeared.

Once over the bridge I headed south through the Palisades Interstate Park. Admiring the river from the high vantage point provided by this mountain road, I could see the wide water sparkling below, and busy towns all up and down its banks. After a few minutes the road began to descend, and I was surprised to feel a sick sensation in my stomach. I don't normally get carsick, and the road wasn't even very winding. Still, there was no arguing with the fact that the farther I descended, the tighter my stomach became. "Must be the excitement," I thought to myself.

At some point the main road flattened out, and I almost drove past a suburban-looking street off to the left. Turning sharply onto it, the first thing I saw was a run-down church, with a sign out front proclaiming "Redemption is just a heartbeat away." Across the street were railroad tracks and beyond that, the river, dominated by the Indian Point nuclear power plant looking over from the other side.

The parts that I could see consisted of two huge concrete domes, and a tall needle of a tower with a stripe of red near the tip, sprouting between them (fig. 1.1). The complex was so clearly shaped like a penis

Fig. 1.1. Indian Point Energy Center (Photo by Tony Fischer)

and testicles that even the word *phallic* seemed like a euphemism. The plant was designed and built in the early sixties; I wondered whether the designers, planners, and politicians involved with the plant's construction could all have been unaware of this blatantly sexual image, or if they had built it that way on purpose as some kind of a public joke. It was unsettling.

I noticed the sick feeling again in my stomach and decided to continue down the road. It ran for a mile or two through a tiny suburban enclave that seemed caught out of time. The houses in Jones Point were few and modest, and many were in disrepair. Overall the street gave a feeling of rural poverty—more like Appalachia or remote Vermont than one of the wealthiest counties in the state. All of the houses shared a beautiful view of the Hudson—and with it, the power plant looming on the opposite shore.

Before that plant was built, this must have been a beautiful place. Sandwiched as it is between the river and the mountains behind it, the village can never have been larger than the few blocks it covers now. Jones Point feels almost like one of those fishing villages you can still see traces of in the Hamptons or in Maine—deriving its power and its character from the water at its doorstep. In the years when the spit of land called Indian Point was a leisure park for steamboat travelers, the view from Jones Point would have been of picnickers and swimmers, artists and writers.

But with the nuclear power plant—not to mention a garbage treatment plant and some other unidentifiable smoking tower also within view—the village felt surrounded by demons. Later I would discover that Jones Point had once been a harbor for retired warships; this grandness would have suited the scenery perfectly, but it made the current bleakness all the more depressing in contrast.

I thought of the people living here, who had seen their beautiful village decay over time, and how they must feel looking out every day at belching smokestacks. I thought of children growing up in the shadow of the plant, then recalled a friend's story of how she often visited a beach near here in the early sixties when she was a child. One day she and her sisters came upon thousands and thousands of dead fish in the shallows and washed up on the shore. Up and down the beach, as far as their eyes could see, dead and dying fish. They didn't understand what had caused the mass die-off, but the image stays with them—and now with me—to this day. Now we know that Indian Point generates a "thermal plume" each time it gets turned on after a period of inactivity. This plume heats up stretches of the river, periodically killing thousands of native fish, plants, and insects, causing the mass die-offs like the one my friend had seen.[2]

Back at the main road, I decided to continue southward to other towns that lived in plain view of the plant. I wondered if they would have the same depressing and sickening effect on me. As it turned out, they didn't. Other towns with equally close views of the power plant did not share the bleak atmosphere of Jones Point. Instead, they seemed more like the middling-to-fancy suburban neighborhoods in the rest of Rockland and Westchester Counties: proud, well appointed, and sophisticated, with property values that reflected their proximity (thirty to forty miles) to New York City.

What could explain this difference? Part of the problem was certainly geographic: Jones Point was really hemmed in by the mountain behind it, and therefore cut off from easy access to neighboring towns. It had that "wrong side of the tracks" feel. But perhaps there was more than one kind of isolation at work here. The Chinese art of feng shui analyzes the way energy moves—or fails to move—through a landscape or building; it is Chinese medicine for very large "bodies." In the case of Jones Point, the river provides a very tangible picture of the flow of the area's energy, and the most striking thing about this part of the river is how little flow there actually is. North of Jones Point, the river rushes through the fifteen miles of canyon that compose the Hudson Highlands. With mountains on either side restricting its course, the river through the Highlands is deep, narrow, and fast. Dutch sailors in the seventeenth century called this stretch of river the "Devil's Horse Race" because the narrowness of the channel coupled with the speed and unpredictability of its current made sailing through it a dangerous and often fatal enterprise.

But the button of land whose tip is Jones Point marks the place where the riverbed makes a hard turn. The rushing water collapses into a wide and shallow bay, and the current slows down. Tides pushing up from the south lose some of their force three miles below, where the river makes another hard turn, so the small strip of coast that holds both Jones Point and Indian Point is nearly a stagnant pool. One analysis estimates that a free-floating log could take three weeks to make the 153-mile journey from Troy to New York harbor, because the water spends almost as much time meandering upstream as it does going down.[3]

Stagnant energy is not a good thing in Chinese medicine, which equates movement and change with life. This backwater energy between Indian Point and Jones Point meant that any poisons or problems would accumulate, rather than naturally washing away. This stagnation would then weaken the regions above and below it by preventing the smooth flow of resources to and from a large stretch of landscape. Even if there were no overt problems at the power plant (many of which have been documented in the forty years since the reactors came online), the overbearing appearance of the power plant and the garbage treatment plant would dominate the small village, undermining its strength and its pride.

To make matters worse, the highway and the mountains behind Jones Point, which keep it so physically isolated, also prevent any negative energies from moving away through the air. Even a strong wind could not clear the place out. In Taoist culture and feng shui practice, it is a given that imbalanced energy in the landscape can adversely affect the human inhabitants. The illness might manifest physically, economically, socially, environmentally, or all of the above, but the underlying cause in each case would be the stagnating toxins of Indian Point.

A practitioner of feng shui would want to make alterations in the environment in order to address the energy imbalances and thereby improve the health and well-being of the people who live in that environment. In ancient times, the emperor might have channels dug to alter the course of a river, or a temple built to cultivate a more harmonious landscape. Nowadays, home and business owners might add particular trees or rocks to their landscaping to change the flow of energy, or rearrange furniture in the house. But all of these fixes are directed at harmonizing the energies of a landscape that is just a little out of balance; feng shui does not have a model for land that has been chronically poisoned.

Driving home that afternoon I felt overwhelmed and depressed, though less sick after ascending out of the valley. I realized that without consciously looking for it, I had in fact stumbled upon the place of the dragon's bad breath. The phrase didn't even seem like a whimsical metaphor anymore, just the truest description I could imagine of the pall I'd experienced that day.

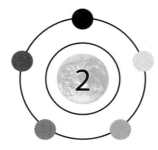

The Pulse of the Land

I woke up thinking about the pulses of the Earth; it was a strange concept. In my acupuncture practice, I place three of my fingers on a person's wrist to take his pulse. Each finger feels something different, and the separate pulses combine together to form a picture that leads to diagnosis. I wouldn't have imagined that this small gesture could be transposed to something as big as the Hudson River, yet Venerable Dhyani had suggested that I listen to pulses three, six, and nine miles away from the power plant. Could these mileage landmarks somehow be analogous to the pulse locations under my three fingers (fig. 2.1)? If that was the case, I would feel different pulse qualities at each mileage point, and these qualities would reflect the health of the area. If I could take pulses at these positions on both banks of the river—as though

Fig. 2.1. In Chinese medicine, three fingers feel the pulse of the radial artery on each wrist.

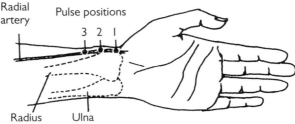

they were a client's two wrists—I might be able to form some kind of a diagnosis.

I rummaged through a box of maps, looking for a detailed image of Westchester County that would include the area around Indian Point. But as I pulled the map from the box, I began to wonder why I was doing it; if what I wanted was to build a stone circle, why didn't I just go build one? Pulse taking might just be a distraction. As soon as I had formulated the thought, however, I understood the reason: *pulse taking is the diagnosis, stone circle is the treatment.* Just as I would never stick acupuncture needles in someone's body without first carefully questioning them and then formulating a diagnosis and a treatment plan, I would not be building a stone circle to help heal the river without doing a lot of preliminary diagnostic and planning work. Though I had intuitively understood from the start that a stone circle would be healing for the river, I hadn't really recognized that I would be performing a treatment. But now it was obvious: the stone circle project was medicine. More specifically, it was acupuncture. Acupuncture for the Earth. And I was to be the acupuncturist.

With that sobering thought in mind, I spread out the map of Westchester and found a ruler. After comparing the ruler to the map's scale of miles I began to look for a few places that were three, six, and nine miles away from the plant. There were so many possibilities; wherever I chose to point the ruler just seemed random. Then I remembered an old drawing compass in the cookie tin that had once been my grandfather's toolbox. With an ancient nub of pencil still in it, the compass was exactly what I needed. Setting it at a length that corresponded to three miles on the map, I quickly drew a circle around the power plant, then two more at six and nine miles away. Looking at my handiwork, I saw I had drawn a huge target, with Indian Point at its center.

The image reminded me of an acupuncture technique called Surrounding the Dragon, which is a method of treating localized physical problems by circling them with needles. In this context, the dragon was the power station, and I could suddenly see it in my mind belching smoke and breathing fire with evil intent, like a fairy-tale monster. The dragon's bad breath again; that metaphor was surprisingly persistent!

Looking at the circles I had drawn, I tried to imagine how I could turn these huge swaths of territory into something whose pulses I could listen to. A lot of the three-mile circle went through a National Guard base. A year after 9/11, I couldn't see myself showing up at the military base with a big map that showed a nuclear power plant at the center of its penciled-in target. Nor could I imagine listening to pulses in the

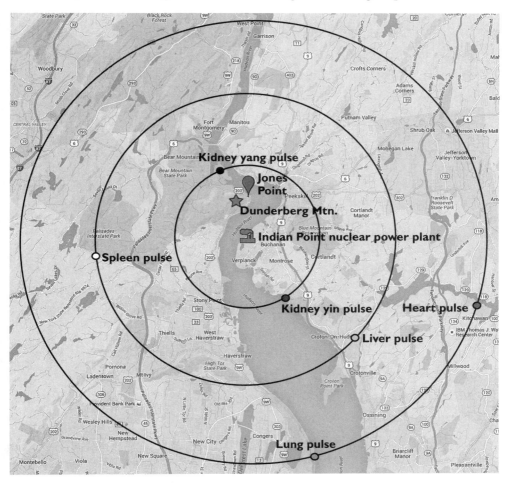

Fig. 2.2. The pulse points at three, six, and nine miles
away from the power plant

middle of a city street, even though a large part of my circle also ran through the cities of Peekskill and Ossining, New York.

I decided to focus on parks and public spaces, where I wouldn't feel so conspicuous. This choice narrowed my options considerably, and I was able to pick out a few spots on the three-mile circle that looked promising. Excited to get going, I had to remind myself that I needed to eat breakfast and be on my way to the office; the pulses I'd be feeling today would be human ones, not riverine.

It is a magical experience, on any day, to listen to another person's pulse in the framework of Chinese medicine. Where modern Western medicine teaches its practitioners to count a pulse in beats per minute, the ancient art of Chinese medicine teaches me not just to measure but to *listen*—to apprehend the broader music of a pulse in qualities of strength and flow that are as variable as waves. I listen with my fingers to discern the subtle currents; with just the right amount of pressure, the tips of my fingers feel like they're rising and falling as each beat passes through. What runs beneath my fingers is quite like a river— sometimes wide and strong and sometimes thin or hollow or slippery.

Some pulses feel as taut as a guitar string, others soft and spongy. Chinese medicine has a whole vocabulary for describing the qualities of pulses—twenty or thirty or sixty words like *thready, wiry, bounding, hollow, weak, slippery, reedy, deep,* and so on. Some teachers believe that a student can't properly feel the pulses until she's learned the words for them; others will have their students feeling pulses for months before the words are even introduced. But whether you learn the words first or the feelings first, the distinct types of pulses soon begin to emerge beneath your fingers. You listen until you can match a particular pulse to a quality you understand.

In my treatment room, I listen with such intense focus that everything around me seems to disappear. Even the sense of "me" disappears as I become one with the pulse. In that still minute, all boundaries dissolve. Everything shifts. When I return to myself, I can never tell how long I was absorbed in that timeless space: was it thirty seconds? A minute? Five minutes? Never mind. What happened in that interval is that time itself yawned: it opened and stretched and gapped. In those interstices of time the rules are different: anything can happen; healing happens.

In my acupuncture office, listening to pulses is an important part of the general listening that I do to understand what's going on with each client. But pulses of the Earth? I couldn't imagine how the silent, sessile land might generate a pulse—or a story for that matter. How was I going to learn what the landscape needed? I had no idea, but I nevertheless set out the next weekend to give it a try.

I drove toward one of the three-mile places I had identified on the eastern side of the river. Reaching the spot proved harder than I'd expected; though my map showed a clear patch of green that indicated parkland, private houses seemed to surround it and I couldn't find an access road. With several inches of wet snow on the ground, I didn't want to trample around through the brush trying to find the park, either: better to pick another location instead.

Poring over the map, my eyes lit upon the tangle of brooks and ponds that feed the Hudson. They reminded me of a network of blood vessels, branching and perfusing the ground. It occurred to me that waterways don't just *look* like blood vessels—they function like them too—circulating oxygen, nutrients, and minerals through an ecosystem. Perhaps these "vessels" could be my pulse points, analogous to the radial artery that I palpate when I take a client's pulse! With that image in mind, I refocused my efforts on public land with water running through it.

I followed one water system—Furnace Brook—as it wound through subdivisions and parks. Never having been on these back roads before, I just drove around, following the brook as best I could. Coming abruptly into a clearing, I found myself looking down on an inlet beside the river. "Oscawanna Isl.," said the map, although it didn't appear to be an island at all, more like a pool or a bay connected to the river by a single narrow channel.

With a sense of excitement I parked the car and walked to the water's edge. What a surprise! Instead of the churning roll of the river just a few yards away, this bay was peaceful—almost sleepy. Small waves lapped onto the thin strip of beach, dotted by seagulls and ducks enjoying a late-afternoon snack. The early winter sunlight was soft and beginning to glow gold and pink on the water.

I put my hands on the cold wet ground, trying to figure out where to put my fingers in order to hear the pulse. But whether I squatted or bent myself down, I was uncomfortable and couldn't concentrate. I thought about sitting on the ground, but realized I'd be soaked in a matter of minutes. I sat on a low rock and decided to see what I could "hear" with my feet on the ground instead of my fingers.

I made an effort to synchronize myself with the mood and pace of this place, as I do with my acupuncture clients. I took long breaths and slowly calmed my thoughts and movements. I hoped to become a part of the scene around me: serene and subdued. After a while I closed my eyes, as I do when I take a person's pulse. I became keenly aware of the sunlight on my face—not warm on this winter afternoon, but bright— and the gentle sound of the waves against the sand. Seagulls called from far away, the ducks squabbled among themselves, and an image came to my mind of an old brown-skinned woman, rocking in a chair.

I tried to push the image away, so I could listen to the pulse of the place. I wanted something similar to what I felt with my hands on a client's wrist—the regular drumbeat of a pulse. But I wasn't feeling or hearing anything like that at all. . . .Then the thought occurred to me that perhaps this mental picture *was* the pulse. Though not an actual beat that I could count or touch, the woman I pictured was a feeling-note, with a definite shape and tone. And my body felt the way it does when I am listening to a person's pulse—still and fully focused, like a radio attuning to a particular signal.

I tuned back in, and the same image returned easily, the gentle rocking of the old woman's chair like water lapping at the beach. She seemed frail and barely present—lost in reverie but somehow content. I kept watching. In a whisper-quiet voice, this old woman began to speak, telling stories of her childhood. I saw her as a young girl, maybe six or seven years old, running and slamming doors and laughing in the sunshine. I saw her with her mother, and her mother's mother, and a long line of mothers going backward through time, as well as a long line of children going forward. Then I was looking at the old woman again—rocking, remembering—and her image faded from my mind. Watching the bay and hearing the birds and the water, my first thought was of the generations that had seen this river flowing back and forth, back and forth, carrying eons of history with it.

That old woman represented the passage of time, and the humans who had been a part of this region for millennia. A brown-skinned woman, in particular, represents to me the first mother, the archetypal mother—a symbol of the earth itself. The fact that she seemed tired and frail was a sign of her role: she had been there from the beginning.

I tried to relate what I'd seen to Chinese medical terminology. If that old woman was a pulse, she was certainly a weak one. I ran through the various pulse patterns in my mind—intermittent, thin, feeble. But her memories: they were a part of her, too, and they were not feeble. They were deep, and they were quiet, but they represented a genuine source of strength. I settled on deep, weak, and thready. This place had inner strength somewhere, but it was not currently accessible.

A weak pulse is, like it sounds, one that beats without a lot of force. On a graph a weak pulse would look like a low-amplitude wave. A thready pulse feels like a thin little string pulling itself along under my fingers, uneven and somewhat fragile. Though it sounds crazy to Westerners, I'm actually listening to twelve different pulses when I take a person's pulse. The twelve pulse positions are considered to be direct reflections of the twelve organ systems that lie at the heart of Chinese medicine. Some practitioners regularly listen to eighteen or thirty-six different positions. For my work with the river, I would simplify this down to six pulses, three on the left bank and three on the right.

In this simplified system, Oscawanna Island—the three-mile

Left hand

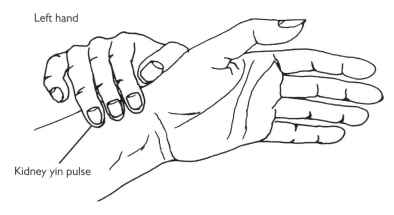

Kidney yin pulse

Fig. 2.3. The pulse point closest to the river mirrors
the pulse point closest to the client's heart.

position closest to the river on the eastern shore—was analogous to the
Kidney yin pulse, which normally runs under my ring finger and closest
to the client's trunk (fig. 2.3).*

In the elaborate cosmology of Chinese medicine, the kidneys manifest the energy we bring into the world with us when we're born, known
as our Source Qi, or Essence. Essence comes from our ancestors; it is
passed down to us through our parents, and it guides our growth and
development throughout our lives. The kidneys give us our sense of
purpose and the will to fulfill our unique destiny.

In the body, Kidney energy divides into the two great poles of Taoist
reality: yin and yang. Kidney yin expresses the fundamental quality of
Essence and the sense of purpose; it nourishes, moistens, and seeds the
organs with an understanding of inner strength. Kidney yang manifests
the growth aspect of being alive—the steadily vibrant furnace known
as the Source Qi or Life-Gate Fire. In the pulse-reading systems that I'd
been taught, Life-Gate Fire is housed in the right kidney, while Kidney
yin is stored in the left kidney. Their pulses are found on the right and

---

*This presumes that the river is like a client lying north to south, facing me: the eastern
shore is the left "hand," and the western shore is the right hand.

left wrists, respectively, in the last position—about two inches from the crease of the wrist. The pulse I had heard was thus a measure of the strength of the river's Kidney yin; its Essence and sense of purpose.

I could see that the old woman's memories were her ancestral energies; they housed her awareness of where she came from and showed this awareness to be an inner strength. But the overall energy of this point was clearly weak—that thin thread of ancestral strength was almost all she had. She knew where she came from but had no sense of forward movement, no sense of purpose. In people, Kidney yin gets depleted from overwork, insufficient rest, and chronic stress; was it possible that the Hudson was weak from overwork and unable to supply itself with a sense of purpose?

A tired river was a sad idea, but not a surprising one. Considering the stresses the Hudson has endured for the past two hundred years, exhaustion might be an appropriate response. Like most rivers near major metropolitan areas, the Hudson River had been a highway for commerce and industry since Robert Fulton's steamboat—widely considered to have inaugurated the beginning of the industrial revolution—ran its maiden voyage on the Hudson in 1807. Since then, countless factories, tanneries, processing plants, and an iron foundry have contributed their effluent to the river. Large-scale dumping of toxic chemicals like PCBs has been common for more than a hundred years, and studies since the 1850s have found sewerage and pollutants that threatened fish and bird populations along the watershed.[1]

The waste from the Indian Point power complex, however, tops all the other sources in volume and toxicity. In the forty-five years since the first reactor at Indian Point came online, the nuclear power plant has dumped thousands of gallons of radioactive waste directly into the Hudson, into the ground at its banks, and into the surrounding air. Some of this has been the legal "allowable" discharge, and some of it has been from countless accidents and malfunctions.

A sampling of such accidents, as reported by state and federal monitoring agencies, includes the following: Radioactive releases into the air and/or water were detected in 1974, twice in 1977, 1980, 1985, 1986, 1992, and 1993.[2] In 1994, one of the Indian Point reactors was found to have been leaking 150 gallons a day for four years—over 200,000 gallons in total.

A leak in 1995 released another 28,000 gallons of radioactive water into the Hudson, and a steam release into the air in February of 2000 caused a full-scale alert.

In 2006, officials revealed that two radioactive isotopes—strontium-90 and tritium—had been leaking into the groundwater at an unidentified rate for an unidentifiable number of years. Even when the plant is functioning perfectly, however, its cooling system sucks in *2.5 billion gallons of river water a day*[3]—and spits it back out hotter and more polluted. No wonder the river is tired. It can hardly fulfill its sacred purpose of cleansing and renewing the landscape when the toxic load upon it is so great.

Strengthening weak Kidney energy is a long process in Chinese medicine, but not an impossible one. The first steps usually include periods of rest and a reduction of damaging activities, as well as herbs and acupuncture. I couldn't imagine how to effect such changes for the river; in what sense would a stone circle—or anything I might do— change this fundamental equation? I had no idea, but I was interested enough, now, in the diagnostic part of the project that I wanted to keep going. I would worry about the treatment later.

The next step of my diagnosis was to find the six-mile pulse on this side of the river. This position would correspond to a person's Liver pulse (fig. 2.4). Where the kidney is the body's source of energy, the liver is more like the programming that keeps the organism function- ing efficiently. In people, the liver is said to govern the smooth flow of energy, blood, and emotions. Its intricate machinery gets gummed up by excesses of heavy foods, feelings, hormones, and inhaled or ingested chemicals, among other things. These excesses create stagnation—and ultimately illness—in our bodies.

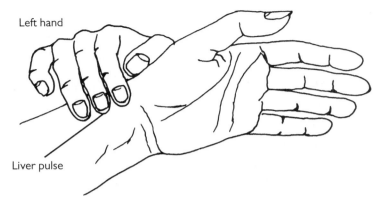

Left hand

Liver pulse

Fig. 2.4. The middle position on the left hand is the Liver pulse

On the six-mile circle, I found only two places on the east side of the Hudson where the circle crossed water. One, a part of the Croton reservoir system, was well below street level and difficult to reach. The other was the Croton River, which had a small narrow park alongside it just at the six-mile mark. Perfect.

As I entered the park, I found myself in a long parking area, empty except for one station wagon all the way at the end. A family was playing touch football nearby, running and shouting and laughing. As I stepped out of my car, the sound of their voices brought a smile to my face; whatever pulse I was going to find here, I knew that at least there'd be some strength in it. That frolicking family was a clear manifestation of healthy energy.

I made my way down a small ravine and came up close to the river. It was roaring. I leaned against a tree and closed my eyes, breathing in the smell of the wet woods. The noise of the rushing water was nearly deafening and obliterated the sounds of the nearby family, birds, and everything else. I was impressed by the energy of this place, so strong and so different from the frail wash of Oscawanna. This stretch of river seemed quite healthy in comparison.

After a few moments, however, the rushing of the water started to make me nervous. I felt like I could be washed away and had to keep opening my eyes to be sure the ground I stood on was safe. I saw branches and debris racing past me, and the river looked churlish and muddy. When I closed my eyes again I imagined a flood, sweeping everything, including me, into its racing waters. I felt afraid.

With surprise I realized that the energy of this place was overbearing; I needed to get away from it. Back in the parking area, which was now quiet, I thought about my experience. I hadn't really heard or seen much that could be called a pulse; I'd been frightened away by the overbearing quality of the place before I'd had a chance to deeply listen. But a pulse is meant to reflect the health of something larger—the organ system it represents. Perhaps I could read that reflection in more than one way. If that were the case, then the overbearingness *was* the pulse, was a legitimate reflection of the river's Liver energy.

Interestingly, excessive force is a common trait of Liver pulses in human beings. When the liver is overloaded, the pulse can get big, wiry, tense, tight, or choppy, among other things. In this case the most appropriate description was *flooding*. Not that the river was actually flooding, but that it was like a flooding pulse, which rushes by the fingers in a big, sort of sloppy way—slightly uncontrolled. It's a sign of a liver in a state of excess.

Again, this made sense to me. With the amount of indigestible and inorganic pollution in the Hudson, its liverlike machinery could easily be overloaded. Perhaps the river just couldn't process the amount of material that was being fed to it. The slow-moving water I'd seen at Jones Point showed clear evidence of stagnation, and now I could understand this stagnation from a Chinese medical point of view: the system responsible for its smooth flow was compromised.

I was surprised at the way the pulse of this area—which I had decided would correspond to the liver—was so similar to common Liver pulses in my clients, just as the river's Kidney pulse was like actual Kidney pulses I had felt dozens of times. Though I had been told that the Earth's body was like a human body, I thought the expression was a metaphor. I hadn't really expected the similarities to be so literal.

The connection was unsettling, but also exciting. The fact that I was so surprised by the pulses I felt actually boosted my confidence in myself and the pulse-taking process; if I were skewing the results or making them up, I reasoned, I would have invented something much less specific. Instead, these humanlike pulses of the Earth were sort of freaking me out, upending all my notions of what it means to be embodied, what it means to have a pulse in the first place.

As I walked back to the car, a deep silence came over me, and I moved and thought in sync with my surroundings. Not too speedy, not too loud. A natural part of the landscape. I felt like I had really *listened* to the land, the way I listen to my clients, and had allowed its experience to temporarily become my own.

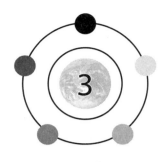

Yin and Yang

In my treatment room, I listen to all the pulses at once to get a sense of the body as a whole, before focusing my attention on the separate wrists and their specific pulse positions. On the river, though, I was limited to one pulse position at a time, because they were miles apart from each other. After listening to two pulse points on the eastern side of the river, I was itching to cross over to the other shore and listen to some pulses there.

My first goal was to find a Kidney yang pulse to complement the Kidney yin I'd palpated at Oscawanna Island. But as I thought about Kidney yang—the Life-Gate Fire—I realized that I felt somewhat ill equipped to find it. My energy is so yin and internal—things that burn and effervesce with constant yang energy mystify me. I keep wondering when they're going to quiet down. I began to think that I needed a yang person to help me discover the yang of the landscape.

The balance of yin and yang is the organizing principle of Chinese medicine and of Taoist thought—as fundamental as science is to Western medicine. Much more than a standstill of forces, balance is about the relationship between the forces—how they give and take with one another, transform and transmute one another, create and control each other in a continuous dance whose net effect is blandly described as balance. Furthermore, the interaction of the two primary forces—yin and yang—creates a whirling dynamo that gives birth to the rest of the world: to the "ten thousand things" as they are described in Taoist classical literature. I realized that in working alone, I had been neglecting the wellspring of energy that arises when yin and yang meet.

The idea of having another person listening to pulses with me was appealing in other ways as well; though I'd had profound experiences with the landscape, I was nervous to be sitting by myself in these out-of-the-way places, deep in meditation with my eyes closed. I did not feel completely safe. I would feel better with another person along to help me—both to guard me as I sat and to help me tease meaning out of the experience.

So who could I ask to join me? Who could be the yang to my yin?

It was a short list of friends who would not think me crazy for trying to listen to the pulses of a landscape. Three, maybe four possibilities. But the two women on my list seemed not to have the right energy from the start; they were too yin, too much like me. My mind turned to James, a fellow acupuncturist with whom I had traded a few treatments. I had become friendly with James and his wife, Laura, over the past couple of years, and we had discovered a lot of common interests. James had recently graduated from the same acupuncture school that I had attended years before, so we spoke the same language of Chinese medicine. I also knew that he had a deeply spiritual side, and I had a hunch that he would understand my interest in helping the Hudson River.

I thought about asking James and Laura together, but quickly realized that Laura—who was trying to get pregnant—should not be involving herself with a nuclear power plant. No matter; the simplicity of a man-woman team felt exactly right. When doing sacred work there's a special beauty in balancing male and female energies: the yin and the yang complement and support each other, without overpowering. I felt comfortable with James, and he seemed like someone who would understand and enjoy my project. And being an acupuncturist, he would not need any tutoring in pulse taking.

I asked James to meet me one day after work, and over tea I explained the outlines of my project. "I'm not sure I really understand the concept of the land having pulses," he said, twisting a little nervously in his seat, "and not sure how much help I would be, but I'd like to come along anyway." The idea intrigued him, as did my larger goal of helping to heal the river. As he and Laura lived just a few miles from Indian Point, they were quite aware of its poisonous effect on the nearby environs. In fact, they were developing their own plan for improving the health of Peekskill, their hometown: they were planning to open a coffee shop to foster a greater sense of community in their economically depressed city. I sighed with relief at hearing this. James was a healer in his own right and would be bringing his own strengths to the stone circle project. Immediately I felt less alone.

As we stood to leave the restaurant, I was reminded that James was my physical opposite—tall and lanky to my short and round; we looked like Laurel and Hardy. Our physical natures suggested a good balance of opposites, and I felt pleased to have found an appropriate partner for this work.

The following week, I brought James to Jones Point as a way of orienting him to my vision of the power plant and my work thus far. As we drove down the hill toward the point, I noticed a nauseous feeling in my gut and tried to make sense of it. An area below my rib cage felt tight and stuck; perhaps it was my diaphragm—a muscle that often causes nausea when it becomes constricted. I also felt a small throb across the back of my skull. I have learned to cope with my extreme sensitivity by reading my body like an instrument. As long as I am not caught up in some anxiety or distraction of my own, the spontaneous blips and pings of my body—its various buzzes, pains, and constrictions—are surprisingly accurate indications of disharmony in the people or places around me.

In this case my internal sensors were nearly off the scale: the air felt clipped or thin or just *wrong* somehow. I asked James if he noticed anything unusual. He said he found himself sniffing the air a lot, as though he were testing for a smell of something burning or poisonous. "I don't actually smell anything strange," he clarified, "but my body keeps wanting to sniff." Down by the railroad tracks, James was depressed, as I had been, by the overwhelming presence of Indian Point across the bay. "It's like a giant is giving us the finger," he said, noting the spindle tower between the two domes. I told him how the tower had looked to me like a penis and testicles; both images were overbearing and obnoxious.

"What about those architects and urban planners who devote their lives to creating inspiring and beautiful cityscapes?" James asked thoughtfully. "Could such a person have created something less awful here?" It was an interesting question that led me to imagine a fairy-tale castle in place of the domes. Turrets and gingerbread, something evocative instead of provocative. The image made me smile and made me grateful for James's presence. His eager yang energy was already a good counterpoint to my yin internality. Whereas I mostly dreamed of returning the land to its primal state, James could imagine building a different reality; that was healthy yang in action. Of course, a pretty castle leaking radiation wouldn't be much better than what was here now, but a design team that thought about beauty could be one that thought about sustainability, too. The idea seemed radical, but not impossible.

We drove along the short street and talked about the dead-end, downtrodden feeling of Jones Point. James agreed that a lot of the problems seemed to be geomantic ones—the slow-moving bay, the high mountains behind us, and the narrow-necked outlet all contributed to a feeling of backup and stagnation. He also pointed out how different this area felt from Peekskill, just across river. Though it is a poor and run-down city right next to Indian Point—and sitting on the same bay—Peekskill's waterfront feels peaceful and lovely. A long park beside the river hosts many people at play on any given day. Something besides proximity was causing the particular sickness and claustrophobia of Jones Point; why did it feel so much more ill than every place around it? To call this the place where the dragon exhales its bad breath was simply another way of describing the problem, but what could be done about it?

On a bitter cold January day, James and I met at Iona Island, the place I had selected as the three-mile pulse point on the western side of the

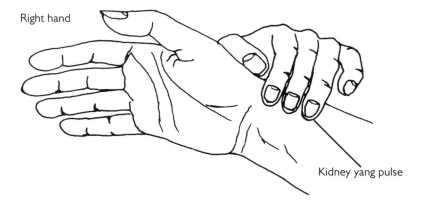

Right hand

Kidney yang pulse

Fig. 3.1. The Kidney yang pulse: Life-Gate Fire

river (fig. 3.1). Iona is a six-thousand-year-old tidal marsh that juts out into the Hudson just below Bear Mountain. A national sanctuary for wild birds, the island is home to many species, including mute swans, Canada geese, mallards, and overwintering bald eagles, as well as many smaller birds, including the tiny heron called a least bittern. In this marsh, saltwater from the Atlantic, which surges upriver with every tide, mixes with freshwater from the upper Hudson and a local brook with the fanciful name of the Doodletown Bight. The brackish result is a six-and-a-half-mile swath of territory that supports more than 450 kinds of plants, animals, and insects.

Walking along the causeway that runs the length of the island, James and I were soon surrounded by tall grasses and profound silence. Though not more than a quarter mile from the highway, we were sheltered from the sounds of traffic by trees and frozen marshland. Days of single-digit temperatures had frozen solid the shallow pools and swamp bottom all around us; delighted, James and I stepped out onto ice. My boots crunched the snow beneath me as I navigated carefully around grasses and stems, not wanting to crush anything. In warmer weather this marshland teems with life; now it was motionless, caught out of time. The water didn't lap, nothing made a sound. Absorbed by a sense of magic in this unfamiliar terrain, James and I wandered separately for many minutes. Head and ears covered against the cold, my breathing was loud and rhythmic inside my hood, and I felt like an astronaut on a moonwalk. I lay down on the ice and peered in at frozen bugs, stems of plants, water bubbles, and seaweeds in a perfect underwater tableau. There was a whole other universe in there.

We met up and decided to explore the interesting turreted ruins at the end of the island. They were fenced off, however, and we weren't willing to flout the No Trespassing signs to get any closer. The place looked creepy, like Frankenstein's laboratory or a small prison. My hiking guidebook said this island had been a huge munitions depot for the first half of the twentieth century, supplying most of the country's ammunition for World Wars I and II. Somehow every glimpse of paradise around here had its dark edge.

We walked a little way back toward the causeway and found ourselves in a small clearing—like a little skating rink among the frozen reeds. We agreed that this was a perfect spot to take a pulse. Emboldened by the fact of having a companion, I had brought along tools this time—a blanket to sit on, cornmeal to offer to the earth, incense to offer to the sky, and a small quartz crystal that Venerable Dhyani had given me at a recent seminar. I hoped the crystal would help me remember my mission with clarity, as well as carry encouragement from Venerable Dhyani and her lineage of earth-healing ancestors.

My freezing fingers struggled to light the sage and cedar incense, then curled around the small crystal as we watched the smoke rise into the gray winter sky. I said a prayer to the spirits of this lovely island, thanking them and the Creator for allowing us to visit here. I offered cornmeal to the birds and grasses, to the water, and to the earth, and stated my intention to listen to the pulse of this place. Then I sat down and closed my eyes, grateful for James's presence, which took away that slight sense of foolishness that I'd felt on my own and helped me feel more powerful. We were proving to be a good team.

Allowing my breath to be free and easy I focused my senses on my surroundings and settled in to listen for a pulse. I felt the cold pinch my nose and smack against my body even through the down coat and wool blanket. The silence was thick. This time, I didn't see a person. I saw the marsh itself, grasses whistling in a spring wind and birds wheeling through the air. Bubbles of gas percolated up through mud, and hundreds of different nests held watchful parents and precious eggs of many shapes and sizes. I saw the marsh as a giant and generous organ—a filter secreting and releasing salt and other minerals to the surrounding ecosystem. The marsh swung and dipped with the high and low tides, adjusting water levels and chemical compositions as needed.

In my mind's eye, eggs hatched and hundreds of birds were born, released into the air like so many butterflies. The marsh provided food and shelter to the hatchlings and their guardians, as well as to the countless fish, reptiles, mammals, and insects that made up the living community of this place. Then autumn came and the birds flew off. Nests decayed and life slowed down, drawing itself deep into the roots of the riverbed. The marsh froze over, saving its precious resources like medicines for the distant spring. Everything was still and cold.

I began to be aware of my own body again, still and cold as well. The freeze had penetrated my bones so deeply that they hurt. It became a symbolic cold, an archetype of cold as much as a personal experience. In Chinese medicine, cold is the climate that relates to the kidneys, and to the bones as well. I realized that many elements of the pulse I'd just taken also suggested the kidneys. Whereas Oscawanna Island had been the river's Kidney yin, it's storehouse of essence and ancestral resources, this point on the west bank of the river seemed—miraculously—to actually reflect Kidney yang. The high density of wildlife here, and its diversity, demonstrated a strong life force—a strong Life-Gate Fire. In fact, this bird sanctuary was literally a life gate: an entrance into life for the hundreds of species that were bred and born here.

In a functional sense, too, marshland is very much like a kidney: they both filter water to remove minerals and impurities, gleaning nutrients in this process that then become available to other parts of the body/ecosystem. Where the kidneys control blood and water pressure in the body, marshland accommodates the changing water and salinity levels of the tides and the seasons, creating fertile ground for new life—another hallmark of the Kidney yang in Chinese medicine. Furthermore, birds are a particularly yang life-form, whose ability to fly up toward the heavens signifies a light and rising yang.

As I filled James in on my pulse reading, he reminded me that one of the essential aspects of the kidneys according to Chinese medicine is their function of storing energy inherited from our ancestors. The cyclical nature of my pulse vision—the circle of seasons—revealed this capacity to store energy. More than satisfied with so much rich Kidney-yang symbolism, we began packing our things to leave. I was distressed to realize I couldn't find the lovely crystal that had been my gift from Venerable Dhyani. Though it had certainly been in my hand as I began the pulse reading, it was now nowhere to be found. Not in my hands, my pockets, the folds of the blanket, or anywhere on the ice that we could see. At first dismayed, I soon began to feel better. The crystal would be my gift back to the ice—back to the spirits of this place that had reminded me of the energy stored within each of us. "Thank you for sharing your crystal wisdom with me," I whispered to the unknown ancestors who filled my kidneys. "I'm so grateful to be a part of your world."

In late January, James and I set out to find the river's Spleen pulse. In Chinese medicine, the spleen is responsible for the transformation and transportation of food and fluid—for extracting energy in the processes of digestion. The spleen separates the basic Food Qi into several more refined forms and transports it to the other organs. Unlike the kidneys, which store the Source Qi that is inherited from our ancestors, the spleen *makes* qi from the foods of the earth. This qi is a renewable resource that powers bodily function on a daily basis: abundant, good-quality Spleen Qi can prevent the Source Qi from becoming drained.

The Spleen pulse is found on the right wrist in the middle

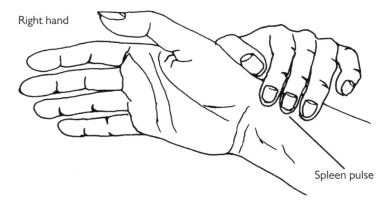

Right hand

Spleen pulse

Fig. 3.2. The Spleen pulse is in the middle position
on the right hand.

position (fig. 3.2). On the river, this corresponded to the six-mile circle on the western side—a good part of which ran through Harriman State Park. The vast 46,000-acre park included several lakes and streams that crossed the six-mile circle, so we headed toward the biggest one. However, as we neared the site, we found the only road blocked off and closed for the winter. No way in. We looked at the map and chose another spot but couldn't get to that one either. It's not uncommon in rural areas to have some roads closed for winter; if they're not frequently used, the expense of plowing and maintaining them is just too prohibitive. Still, it seemed like bad luck to have met with two such roads, and I wondered if this was a reflection of some obstruction of the Spleen Qi.

In the body, Spleen energy becomes obstructed when we eat poorly—keeping irregular mealtimes, eating too much or too late at night, ingesting too many sweets and grains. Quite common as well is a pattern of overactive Liver energy invading the spleen, spreading its stagnation into the digestive system. If the Hudson had obstructed Spleen energy, it was a sign that the river was unable to digest everything that was happening to it.

We eventually found a small stream on the six-mile circle where we could read the Spleen pulse, but it was a tiny little brook by the side of the road, and I felt disappointed. I doubted I'd be able to read much of anything at this unremarkable spot but decided to try anyway, as it seemed the only chance I'd be likely to get. After my prayers to the earth and sky, and cornmeal and sage smoke, I unwrapped a large crystal that I had brought with me today. I had been planning to bathe it in the river. I carefully placed the crystal in the frigid shallows of the tiny stream and watched with amazement as crystal quartz met liquid crystalline water. The two seemed made for each other.

I settled into my meditation and was surprised that the first image that occurred to me was laughter. This little rivulet seemed to be laughing with joy. In my mind's eye I saw a different river—a larger one—in the summer sunshine, with families paddling in the shallows and some older children playing in the current. There was music in the background—the sound of a choir with many beautiful voices lifted in sacred song. The river's current was a speedy one, and the children playing in it were swept rapidly along into a big pool, where they laughed and climbed out to do it all over again. The overall feeling was one of slightly edgy fun.

I returned to the present moment, surprised to find the snow piled all around me because I had just been experiencing summer. I laughed—with the sheer pleasure of the vision, and also with amusement at myself—for having thought that a small stream would be somehow less telling than a larger one. Ha! Wisdom can appear in many different forms.

James told me he also felt joy at this pulse point. He'd been remembering his wedding—the way he and Laura had felt as the day whirled by them, feeling slightly overwhelmed at being surrounded by so many people who loved them. "This is a Spleen pulse, though," he pointed out. "The spleen governs digestion and thought. What do these happy scenes mean in a spleen context?"

Good question. Joy is associated with the heart, not the spleen, in classical Chinese medicine. The spleen is associated with caring and with worry in an imbalanced state. Neither of those seemed to fit. "It's the pacing, I think," James spoke again. "That feeling of things moving a little too fast to grab on to."

"Slippery," I said, after a moment. A slippery pulse is one that rolls under your fingers—"like pearls in a dish of snot," one teacher had described it. A common characteristic of Spleen pulses, slipperiness indicates congestion of fluids and untransformed food. A slippery pulse for the river might not be imbalanced, though; it seemed to me that a river *should be* slightly slippery—it is running water, after all. Pregnant women are supposed to have slippery pulses, too: perhaps certain kinds of congestion are necessary in a being who is nourishing others.

"Don't forget the obstruction," James reminded me. We'd turned away from two blocked roads in order to get here, and this stream, when we finally found it, was a narrow trickle.

"So the pulse is thin and slippery," I said, "and maybe obstructed, too." But there was that clear feeling of joy as well, and although it didn't make sense in our Chinese medical view, it was still a wonderful quality that we didn't want to discount. "And maybe happy, too," I added, letting the mismatch stand. "Maybe happy, too."

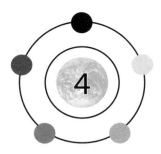

Heaven and Earth

Taoist cosmology describes humans as existing "between" heaven and earth; we absorb the energies of both realms and mix them together, maintaining a complex harmony that mirrors both above and below. The three-part harmony of heaven, earth, and mankind appears in the practice of Chinese medicine as well, defining the origins and interactions of each of these energies. Specifically, Chinese medicine describes three kinds of energy that people acquire from the cosmos: the qi of heaven, which is inhaled by the lungs and mixed with the energy of the heart; Earth Qi, which comes from the foods we eat and is transformed by the spleen; and the qi of humanity—Source Qi—which comes from our ancestors and is stored in the kidneys.

In my pulse readings thus far, I had already assessed the quality of the Source Qi in the kidneys, and the Earth Qi in the spleen and liver. Now I needed to investigate the third important category of the river's qi—the Heavenly Qi of the heart and lungs. The heart and lungs establish the rhythm of our moment-to-moment existence via the breath and the pulse. They regulate the ways that we integrate the energy of heaven into our daily lives.

On March 12, my birthday, I decided I would listen to both the Lung and Heart pulses, thereby finishing the pulse-taking aspect of my project. James was unable to join me on this day, but I found I didn't mind going alone; it seemed like a great way to celebrate my existence.

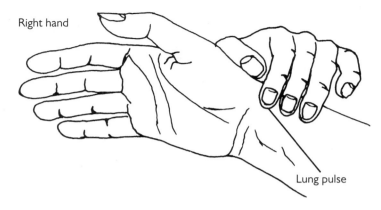

Right hand

Lung pulse

Fig. 4.1. The Lung pulse

I was eager to be out in the fresh air, listening to the landscape with all my might.

Aiming for the Lung pulse first, I drove to Nyack Beach State Park, whose waterfront crossed my nine-mile circle on the western side. On a person, this pulse would be in the first position on the right wrist, under my index finger (fig. 4.1). At the park, I walked along a paved pathway that rolled out beside the Hudson. The river ran straight and wide here, just a few miles north of the Tappan Zee Bridge. A steep sill of the Palisades stretched up on my other side. The season was turning, but the cold air gave no indication. Chunks of river ice still huddled against the shoreline in frozen waves, making odd kinetic sculptures.

At a bend in the path I sat on a good-size rock and looked around. The long, wide expanse of the river sparkled in weak sunlight. It also muttered and groaned as the ice floes bumped and scraped against each other, pushed by the shifting water. I breathed deeply and closed my eyes to the sound of hawks screeching in the air around me. I heard many different bird calls and wished I knew how to identify them.

In my mind's eye I saw a mountaintop wreathed in mist, towering over the landscape below like a scene from a Chinese brush painting. Birds nested in the craggy stone, but this domain was far removed from any sign of humans—or even of trees. The birds went about their business, occasionally winging down through the air on a search for food or simply for the joy of it, then returning to the cliff. Clouds passed into and around each other, forming banks that suggested solidness, then faded away. All was peaceful in this rarified atmosphere, though a little bit . . . severe, somehow.

I opened my eyes to a landscape that was physically very different from the one I had seen in the pulse vision, but similar in tone—cold and grey and spare. Before I could decide what to make of it, two large birds rode into my field of vision, standing poised and straight on an ice floe about thirty feet from where I sat. Some kind of hawk—perhaps immature bald eagles; whatever they were, they looked stern and magnificent as they sailed by, like royals on a journey among the commoners.

I felt a bit like a commoner in that moment, utterly earthbound and concerned with details that must be inconceivable to those lofty beings, focused as they were on the pure dichotomies of stillness and flight, near and far, air and land, life and death. The quest for simplicity and purity is a characteristic of the lungs, I reminded myself. As they separate Heavenly Qi into its component clear and turbid parts (which Western chemistry identifies as oxygen and carbon dioxide), the lungs must cleave the pure from the impure. There is little room for shades of gray here—the organs simply purify what is purifiable and discard the rest.

I could interpret the misty mountain world I'd seen as a symbol of purity and of the heavens. The birds in my vision were like lungs, forever moving between that pristine upper world and the busier one below, as though inhaling and exhaling that pure Heavenly Qi. In that sense, the lungs seemed quite healthy, but I couldn't shake the feeling of something slightly dark and somber here. Uncompromising. In Chinese medicine, a common imbalance of the lungs leads to a kind of overpurification—an arid internal state that leaves the lungs brittle and vulnerable to illness. Perhaps the Lung Qi of the river was a little too harsh in this way.

Satisfied with this pulse reading, though a little saddened by its

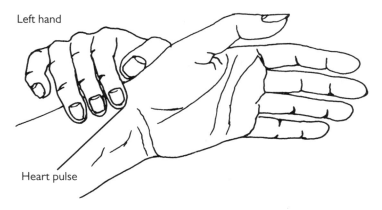

Left hand

Heart pulse

Fig. 4.2. The Heart pulse

austerity, I made my way toward the last pulse point on my list: the pulse of the Heart (fig. 4.2). My map had revealed only one promising spot for this reading, the Kitchawan Reservoir system, where a park and walking trails would lead me close to the water's edge.

The drive to the reservoir took me through a blue waterscape, where bridges spanned lake after sparkling lake, bordered by high snowy hills. I rolled down my car windows to let in the cold blue air and opened my lungs wide to soak up its clean mineral tang. I felt full of joy.

In Chinese medicine, the heart governs the quality and movement of blood, as it does in the West. It also has metaphysical responsibilities, however, housing consciousness and the spirit. The heart governs our ability to be aware of ourselves, to connect to heaven, and to be motivated by divine light. The Heart pulse can reveal the extent to which a person is at peace with herself, and how thoroughly her inner light is integrated with her personality here on Earth. I wasn't sure how these qualities might translate to a pulse on the land, but I was eager to find out.

At least a half dozen cars crowded the slushy parking lot at the reservoir, which was surprising on a weekday morning. As I set out on the path into the park, I noticed a few people coming and going. One woman laughed and swore loudly into her cell phone. A couple ran by with two Irish setters, who barked wildly at some geese in a pond. This set the geese to raucous honking, which excited the dogs even more. Someone whizzed by on a bike. This cacophony was definitely not what I'd expected. Somewhat annoyed, I walked faster, hoping to bypass the Irish setters and find a quiet place. But the park was like a city park—wide open and busy, with few sheltered spots or hidden trails. People were everywhere, in groups and on cell phones, and nothing felt wild or naturelike. My heart sank. Should I leave this park and find another? How could I get a feel for the land when there were so many people around?

Leaving felt wrong, however. If I wanted to understand the land, I needed to see it as it was, not as I wished it could be. I decided I would listen to this place, and not look for a "better" one. Ahead on the trail was a group of large boulders. I circled it to find one side that felt relatively protected and leaned against the cold rock. The winter sun lit my face and prompted me to relax a bit. I listened for a pulse. . . .

Burrowing through layers of people and dogs and noise, my mind finally came to rest in a still spot. Though I'd been annoyed, the land was not. It was calm. Surprisingly calm, in fact, considering the levels of activity here. Almost *too* calm, really, more like passive. This land felt resigned to being used. The word that came to mind was *slatternly,* like a woman who has let herself go. I remembered the complaint of a long-ago client, an actress who found herself typecast into particular kinds of roles. "I'm always the whore with a heart of gold," she said, and I knew immediately what she meant. That's what this pulse felt like.

Whore is a harsh word, and I was disturbed to find myself thinking it. Disturbed even more to think of the Earth in the same breath. The Earth a prostitute? It sounded so judgmental, not to mention heretical. But a whore with a heart of gold is an archetype—sometimes an actual prostitute, but as often a doting mother or an abused wife—someone who gives of herself (and her body) endlessly, from her deepest resources, but who asks for too little in return. This creates a vulnerability in her, a lack of self-protection that leaves her open to more than one kind of abuse.

In a sickening way I now saw the Earth like this. Constantly giving her resources, demanding nothing in return. Stripped of everything—materials, entire species, and respect—yet still offering more. It was a heartbreaking image. For all the times I'd been told that the Earth is a being, I'd never quite believed it. When other people spoke of the planet being abused or raped I thought it was a metaphor—and a melodramatic one at that. Now I saw the Earth as a person and was stricken as much by her degradation as by her beauty. We have nearly used her up.

On the edge of despair, I fought to keep such bleak thoughts at bay. "I'm here to do medicine," I told myself. "Healing works. How can I apply what I know to this situation?" Taking a deep breath I struggled to bring myself back to the basics of Chinese medicine. The systems. The organs. The relationships.

I needed to think about a damaged heart—the core of a person's being and the home of the spirit. The organ of intelligence, consciousness, endurance, compassion, and wisdom. Here feeling weak and resigned, and chronically—globally—disappointed. In Chinese medicine, a heart injured in this way indicates a serious spiritual problem that can easily lead to dangerous physical ones—to conditions recognized by modern medicine as stroke, delirium, and heart failure, for example. One of the ways that Heart Qi can become so weak is if the organ called the pericardium (also known as the heart protector) isn't working properly—if it hasn't fulfilled its job of shielding the heart from shock and betrayal.

I was momentarily surprised to think of the Earth as having a heart protector at all. The heart protector is like a security guard, opening and closing to allow or prevent others from prematurely entering the inner sanctum of the heart. A healthy heart protector turns away from people or energies that feel unsafe or simply unproven; on the other hand, it slowly opens to those who demonstrate a clear record of safe, considerate behavior. The heart protector is the part of us that says no when someone tries to cadge yet another favor, take advantage of our good will, or persuade us into acting against our instincts. It is also the part of us that says yes to becoming vulnerable, to trusting other people, and to falling in love.

If the Earth had a heart protector, then it had the capacity to set boundaries, to say no to the endless tide of human plunder. This was a new thought. Did the Earth have a choice in these matters? Had she been saying yes all these years to our devouring hungers—and would she someday change her mind? It wasn't hard to imagine what a no might look like: floods, storms, earthquakes. We have plenty of those. Or we might see an absence of water, of fertile soils, of viable crops.

Evidently the Earth does say no sometimes, and the destruction can be catastrophic. Though there may be a kind of poetic justice in the Earth's taking back her landscape, nobody wants to see it happen that way. It's just too painful. But would we rather she let the behavior continue? Among our human acquaintances, we *beg* abused people to stand up for themselves and walk away from their abusers. In fact, we expect such refusal as a sign of good mental health. It's quite possible that our planet in a state of recovery may find myriad ways of protecting herself—and we probably won't like them.

So what's the alternative? I don't see us going back to a Stone Age lifestyle—at least, not if we can avoid it. Even as I'm asking the question, though, the answer comes to me clearly. *We need to give prayers of thanks.* We need to respect the gifts of Mother Earth and say "thank you" with humility and grace. Until quite recently in our history, people everywhere said prayers of thanks to the gods of rain and sun, held planting and harvest celebrations, let fields lie fallow, and generally reveled in a partnership with the source of life. It was and still can be a joy to participate in the grand cycles of the seasons, giving as well as receiving, resting as well as working.

In this model, age-old practices of making offerings to the gods actually seem rational: small gifts, prayers, and rituals offer at least something in exchange for the food, minerals, and plants we harvest. Even if the things we give are largely intangible, at least there's a sense of reciprocity behind them. In any relationship—with a person, a dog, our

own creativity—the difference between mutual respect and mutual degradation often comes down to a few small actions, which we regularly
teach to our children but somehow fail to enact in our relationship
with the Earth: Don't take without asking; give something in return
for what you've received; say thank you.

For millennia, humankind followed these rules of relationship with
the Earth. But because we have given up thinking of the Earth as a
being, and think now of an "it" or a factory with endless products available for the taking, we have given up any sense of partnership we may
once have felt. We deride our "superstitious" forebears as though they
were truly stupider than we, because they believed in a living world.
And yet, who would know the true nature of the planet better than
those whose entire lives were engaged with it?

In fact, the more that *I* was engaging with the natural world—the
more time I spent out in the woods, listening to wind and birds and
rustling leaves—the more I was spontaneously rekindling my relationship with the Earth. It was happening quite naturally; all I was doing
was recognizing someone "there" beneath my feet and humming, buzzing, whirling all around me. Maybe part of what the planet needs is just
fewer barriers between the people and the raw material of nature.

I wanted to give something special to this park today—because it
seemed so downtrodden, but also because it had led me to some simple
remedies for problems that had seemed insurmountable. Saying thank
you to the Earth and spending more time outside are simple practices
that many people might be willing to relearn.

I thought of a meditation I had done after 9/11, visualizing the
globe of the Earth in my arms.* I had hugged her, soothed her as a parent might soothe a hurting child. Today I recreated this meditation.
Cradling the Earth in my arms, I imagined her weeping with grief and
disappointment. I pictured her wounds—areas of war and strife and

---

*This meditation is an adaptation of the Medicine Wheel Mandala practice taught by
Venerable Dhyani Ywahoo.

environmental disease—and gave each one a healing kiss, ending at the Hudson River near Indian Point. Then I imagined the Earth's heart. In my mind it was filled with loving people, each one sending out prayers of hope and healing. I wanted the Earth to know she was being cared for, day and night.

With a smile on my face I made my way back to the car. This meditation had freed me from a problem, that of trying to imagine little me talking to or healing something as large as a planet—or even a single river. Sure the Earth is big, but if I can imagine it small enough to hold in my arms, I can relate to it as a being needing love and care like the rest of us. In the realm of the spirit our essential natures have no size or scale. We can be as big as our dreams.

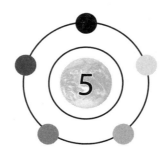

Eagle Dance

I sat staring at the chart I had drawn up of the river's six pulses. I had ascribed a few characteristics to each specific pulse, just as I do with clients in my practice, but the task of bringing them all together into some kind of coherent diagnosis was eluding me. The pulses didn't conform to a classical pattern like Heart Fire, or Liver Invading Spleen; rather, there seemed to be several different imbalances going on at once, and I wasn't sure what to *do* about any of them.

Somehow I needed to make sense of all those pulse readings and collate them into a plan for a stone circle, but I really had no idea of how to get from here to there. I lit a candle and sat down to meditate, asking for guidance on what to do next in my bid to help the river. The answer that came was the image of those two huge birds floating past me on the ice floe. In my imagination, they were staring directly at me with their bright insistent eyes. It was the manner of their looking that struck me most deeply; they seemed to see everything.

As I finished my practice I found that I almost knew what to do next: I needed to see like an eagle. In Native American medicine, as in many traditional systems, different animals represent different forms of wisdom. Eagle Medicine is a medicine of perspective and context, of far-sightedness. It is the opposite of Mouse Medicine, which includes the ability to examine the tiniest details of a thing close-up. Both views are crucial in understanding a situation; the trick is in being able to flow back and forth between them, rather than getting stuck in one mind-set.

After three months of listening to the landscape with mouselike intensity, I was ready for the eagle's-eye view; I just didn't know how to get it. How could I learn to think like an eagle? The answer came almost immediately, and from a surprising quarter. The very next day I was in my office giving an acupuncture treatment. Jane, my client, was lying on the table with her eyes closed, beginning to drift off into a quiet rest. She suddenly opened her eyes and said, "Have you been to see the eagles?"

"No," I answered with surprise. This was a helpful coincidence. "What eagles?" Jane explained that there was a large bald eagle nesting ground not too far from my office, at George's Island Park. Anyone willing to brave the winter air by the riverside in the early morning or late afternoon would be able to see eagles feeding from the river. She had counted sixteen birds the other day.

That was all I needed to hear. I called James that night, and we made a plan to meet at George's Island Park in a few days. Since I was looking for a change in perspective, I didn't want this trip to feel like one of our pulse-reading days. I asked if Laura wanted to come along, and she happily agreed.

George's Island Park was just a few miles south of Indian Point, reached by an access road that was inconspicuously marked right next to the VA hospital. As we entered the park the next afternoon we saw a small road up ahead of us, and a larger road that led off to the left. We took the larger road for a quarter mile or so, to a large empty parking area. When we got out of the car we were struck by the cold winds coming off the river. At the north end of the park was a small grassy area where we decided to stand. We looked around for fifteen minutes or so but didn't see any birds. And we were freezing.

I remembered an eagle dance I had been taught at one of Venerable Dhyani's workshops; over the swirling and swooping movements of the dance, the teacher had guided us to fly over a war-torn region of the world and send waves of compassion and healing. This seemed a perfect thing to do at the moment; I wanted to spread that eagle-eyed compassionate healing energy over the troubled and tumultuous Hudson. I also hoped that the eagle dance might somehow call some eagles to fly our way so we could see them. However, I felt embarrassed to dance in front of James and Laura. I am not a dancer and felt myself to be lacking in grace and skill. I tried to forget about it, but I couldn't get the idea of the dance out of my head; I was itching to do it. So I decided to put my awkwardness aside and just plunge in. I told James and Laura what I was doing, then pulled off my bulky coat, faced east, and began the dance.

Diving and soaring to the four directions, I tried to see the Hudson from an eagle's-eye view. I remembered my original vision, which had unfolded from that kind of high perspective. I felt the cold air and thought about all the people living alongside this great river, helpless to control or even to know of the serious risks the power plant embodied. I thought about the work I had been doing to help the river heal and wondered what my next steps were going to be.

I loved the feel of my limbs sweeping around in the frigid air and was grateful for this physical task of movement, so different from the focused cogitation of trying to figure things out. In this moment, I didn't need to understand; I just needed to fly. As I continued to circle to the four directions I scanned each horizon for signs of eagles, but to my great disappointment, none appeared. Perhaps I wasn't doing the dance well enough, or maybe my mind wasn't clear enough.

After a while I stopped dancing. We searched the sky for a few more minutes, then climbed into the car to warm up. Laura and I were cold, and kind of spent, but James wanted to take the other road—the first one we'd seen when we'd entered the park—and see where it led. My intuitions had thus far not led us to any eagles, so I was glad that James had some ideas. We drove over to the access road and found that it ended abruptly at a wooded area. We parked the car and began to walk in the quiet woods.

As soon as our feet began to crunch on the frozen ground, the woods weren't quiet anymore. We circled through the bare maples and oaks, looking up into the trees for birds. Following James's lead, we found ourselves at the end of the woods, near the frozen edge waters of the river. To the south we could see the little beach where we had just been; where I had done the eagle dance to no avail. We tromped back into the woods, looking for eagles' nests or some other signs of life. Laura pointed out a craggy shape high on a tree branch that she thought might be a bird; we stopped to look.

We stared up into the steely winter sky. Now that we had stopped moving, the silence was thick and compelling. Tall dark trunks and bare branches made angular etch-a-sketch drawings all around us. The three of us stood there, heads stretched back to look at every high branch and dark shadow, hoping to see an eagle materialize. I was reminded of old fairy tales about evil crows and medieval woods that came to life.

Quietly craning, we stared wordlessly into the sky for endless minutes. After a while without conscious thoughts, I had a sudden flash that we had become like eagles ourselves—perched and silent and waiting. No sooner did that thought cross my mind than a great shape lifted out of a nearby tree and rose into the sky above us. Then another, and another. Three bald eagles flew in circles above our heads, rising high but not flying away—three magnificent dancers, mirroring the three of us on the ground. As they wove and spun above us, I realized the birds were answering our call. The minute we had become like eagles, we had spoken their language, and this was them speaking back. I said a silent prayer of thanks to each bird, and to my two friends, whose stillness had helped to create this moment.

After some minutes the eagles flew off, and we walked silently back toward the car. As we left the woods, I slipped on a patch of ice and suddenly found myself laying flat on my back, staring up at the sky again. I had bumped my head hard, but because I was wrapped and hooded against the cold, I had a certain amount of cushioning. It occurred to me as I lay there that maybe my body was trying to tell me something; maybe I needed to be looking at the sky more often—spending still more time as an eagle, less as a mouse.

The eagle and the mouse were just different manifestations of yin and yang, I realized—symbols of earth and sky. Just as the ancient Taoists understood mankind to be continuously modulating between heaven and earth, Native thought has a similar construction. In the Native way, humans stand between Mother Earth and Father Sky, learning to meld the qualities of both realms in wise and loving action. Thus far, I had been very focused on the task of listening to Mother Earth through the pulses; now, perhaps, it was time to visit Father Sky.

James and I decided that the best way to visit the sky—short of flying—was to climb a mountain. We agreed that Dunderberg Mountain seemed like a good choice: it was just across the river from Indian Point and was lined with trails. In late March, the ground was still too icy to be climbing, so we set a date for the beginning of April.

At the foot of Dunderberg Mountain, we sloshed around in the early springtime brush and snowmelt but couldn't manage to find the trail-head. Though clearly described in my hiking book, the trail must have been overgrown, because it completely eluded us. Instead, we found our way to a rocky rise at the foot of the mountain and climbed around on that for a while. It looked like a waterfall of rocks, like a river itself, and we sat inside a rocky cleft out of the wind and surveyed our surroundings.

The ground was damp from melting snow and gave off a rich and loamy smell. Dead leaves from the previous autumn lay everywhere, composted by the winter but not yet crumbled into the new soil they would become. We heard the rustling of squirrels and the persistent trilling of red-winged blackbirds. James remarked how he could really feel the presence of spring approaching—he sensed a new and bright energy uncurling somewhere, ready to transform the world. I heard it as a tune, almost a hum that was higher and faster than the deep tones of winter. Thought this was not quite the hike we'd prepared for, we still felt glad to be in the woods, alongside the earth as it made ready to change.

As we sat on the cold rocks and talked, my eyes kept returning to a particular group of rocks a short distance beyond my feet. One rock in the pile looked like a face, watching us, and I almost wanted to include it in our conversation. Finally I stood up to examine this rock face more closely. The rock was oval and a little bit larger than my hand; it cradled nicely in my palms. The rock did, indeed, look like a face. At least a head, anyway, with a faint suggestion of eyes and a nose. "The eyes of Dunderberg," I called it, even though I could barely make out any eyes. I held the rock on my lap as James and I talked.

"If the Hudson was a meridian," James wondered aloud, "which one would it be?" We pondered the question for a while but came up with no ready answer. In a general sense, every river is like a meridian. Rivers conduct energy along their lengths, connecting the towns and cities that sit upon their shores just as meridians connect the various organs and systems of the body. But organs and meridians have such specific functions in our bodies; could the Earth's landmarks really fit into the same model?

If the river were a part of some larger system, then the whole Hudson Valley would function like an organ within that system. Was it possible to envision our surroundings as some giant stomach or lung, digesting or breathing or governing the smooth flow of energy in the landscape? Maybe. It was an intriguing idea—the country laid out like a giant body with its own organs and meridians and energy systems—but we couldn't quite envision the specifics. Where was the heart? Where the liver? Not to mention the armpits and fingernails and other specific parts. We agreed that expecting our acupuncture metaphor to extend so neatly over every detail felt foolish, as though we were trying to force reality to fit our model. So we let go of that idea and just admired the view, listened to the birds, and got ourselves ready to leave.

"Should I take it home with me?" I asked James, holding up the eyes of Dunderberg rock that I'd been cradling in my lap. The stone was larger and heavier than the kind I might normally pick up as a souvenir, and I felt uncomfortable grabbing on to it as if it were mine to take.

That was the kind of disrespect for the land that I was trying to correct. Still, something in me had made a connection to this particular piece of the world, and I wanted to honor that feeling, too. The only solution I could think of was to ask the rock if it wanted to come home with me. Though I felt incredibly silly, that's what I did.

Of course, I expected no audible answer, and got none. But in the asking I felt open and glad that I had paused to consult the land instead of just taking this piece of it with me. In this open state I felt no resistance to my thought of bringing the eyes of Dunderberg home, only a sense of possibility. When I imagined leaving the rock in its place, I felt nothing. Both choices felt okay. I decided to bring the rock home, vowing that I would return it if I felt uncomfortable with it at home. Before I left, I tipped my water bottle out onto the ground where the rock had lain, as a gesture of thanks. It felt inadequate. After a moment, I pulled a few strands of hair from my head and offered them to the earth. "I look forward to seeing things through your eyes," I said softly. "Thank you."

At my house, I put the rock in a corner of the living room, against a tall, skinny pillar of stone that I had picked up from the low wall around my house. The rock would be my touchstone, I decided—a way to check in with land about my project, to see if my ideas felt right.

That evening, as I wrote down my notes from the day, I felt that the rock was a good companion and a reminder to keep me focused. I imagined it nodding in approval as I carefully described the leafy wet woods, and my own sincerity in asking the landscape for permission to take home this piece of it. Writing the question that James had posed: "If the Hudson were a meridian, which one would it be?" I glanced over at the eyes of Dunderberg, half expecting an answer. The rock sat silently, its face now inscrutable, and I was left to ponder the question on my own.

Exercise I

☀ Creating a Relationship with a Tree

Trees, like humans, are individual beings that exist as part of a collective community. Establishing a relationship with an individual tree-being is a powerful experience and a good first step in becoming conversant with nonhuman awareness.

1. Walk around a park, yard, or woodland and look at the trees around you. Pick out three or four medium-to-large trees and spend a few moments observing each one. Look at their height, width, shape, and colors. Notice the base of each tree and its strong roots.

2. Choose one tree that attracts or intrigues you and walk slowly toward it. Smile in greeting as you approach, and stop three to four feet away from the trunk. Say hello to the tree, silently or out loud. Open your heart and allow the tree to feel your energy.

3. Take a few moments to consider the many contributions this tree makes to its immediate surroundings: the relationship it has with neighboring trees; the oxygen and food it provides to insects, birds, and mammals; the shelter and housing it gives; as well as the shade, beauty, medicine, protection, and recreation it offers to humans. Move a few steps closer and offer your wholehearted thanks to the tree for as many of these services as you can think of in the moment. If you can, sprinkle some cornmeal or raw (unroasted) nuts or seeds at the base of the tree as an offering of thanks.

4. Moving closer still, sit or stand so that your hands or back rest against the tree. Close your eyes and breathe deeply, inhaling the fragrant and richly oxygenated air. Feel the bark under your fingers. Visualize yourself as a companion to the tree, drawing energy up from the earth into your body, as the tree does with its roots, and down from the heavens through the crown of your head, as the tree does through its branches and leaves. Imagine that you are also a tree. Feel the air blowing against your body, the community of life all around you and within you.

5. Greet your friend the tree from this new place of awareness. Ask the tree to show you how it feels. Ask it what it looks at, how far its awareness extends, if it feels any weaknesses or problems. Let the tree's responses come to you, understanding that they may come fleetingly—as visual images, words, colors, sounds, or sensations of many kinds. Spend a few moments experiencing life from the tree's perspective.

6. Ask the tree about its community: who or what are the beings woven into its awareness?

7. Ask about the history of this place. How has the landscape changed since the tree was small?

8. Bring your awareness to the branches and leaves emerging from the top of your body. Visualize them condensing and shrinking into the hairs on your head. Imagine your roots pulling in and becoming the grooves in the skin on the bottoms of your feet. Visualize your bark softening to skin and feel your heart defining your human boundaries again.

9. Sit silently for a few more minutes, once again a human companion to the tree-being beside you. When you feel you are fully yourself, thank the tree one more time—with a nod or a kiss or a gentle touch—and walk away. It is a good idea to revisit your tree from time to time so that you can maintain your relationship.

PART II

Point Location

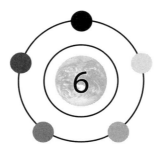

6

The Extraordinary Channels

One day I flipped open my road atlas to ponder the riverscape. Tucked among the pages was a section of newspaper that James and Laura had given me a few weeks previously, which I had forgotten to look at. Unfolding the large paper now, I saw that the main article was about a new display at the Hudson River Museum that presented a thirty-one-foot topographic model of the river and its shores. The exhibit, called the Hudson Riverama, explored the way the Hudson embodies three distinct ecosystems—forestland on the upper part of the river, marshland in the middle section, and estuary in the lower part of the river, which feeds into the Atlantic Ocean. The illustration in the newspaper defined the three sections of the river, color-coding them to show where one ecosystem gave way to the next (fig. 6.1).

This picture triggered an association in my mind . . . three sections. I suddenly realized that I was, in fact, looking at an acupuncture meridian: it was the Conception Vessel, which demarcates three sections of our bodies, known as the lower heater, middle heater, and upper heater (see fig. 6.2 on page 64).*

---

*Another meridian, the Triple Heater, governs the activities of the three heaters, but it is the Conception Vessel's landmarks that define the boundaries of each heater.

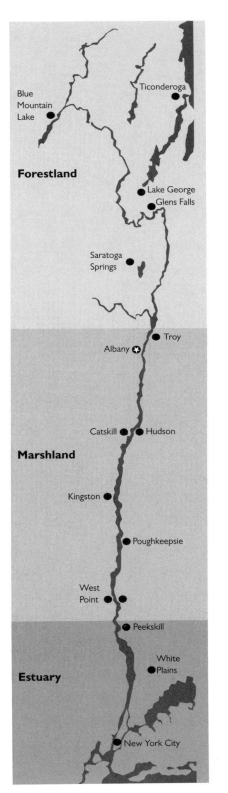

Fig. 6.1. The three sections of the Hudson River: forestland, marshland, and estuary

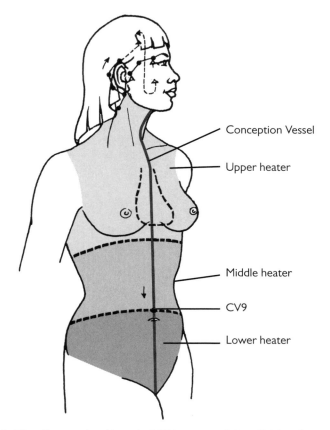

Conception Vessel

Upper heater

Middle heater

CV9

Lower heater

Fig. 6.2. The Conception Vessel of Chinese medicine divides the trunk into three sections known as the three heaters.

At first glance, these three ecosystems of the Hudson looked a lot like the three heaters of the body. I examined the newspaper's rendering more closely. The southernmost part of the Hudson was the estuary region: it was a section that ran from New York harbor up past Indian Point to the Peekskill Bay (fig. 6.3). Estuaries mix seawater with fresh water and are home to many species of plant and animal life that rely on this fertile mix. The article noted that more than two hundred kinds of fish are found in the estuarial Hudson and its tributaries, including striped bass, bluefish, and blue crab. Dozens of birds, mammals, and reptiles also feed on these fish species.

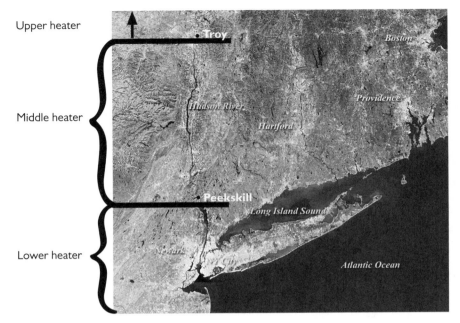

Fig. 6.3. The Hudson's lower and middle heaters
(photo by NASA/GSFC/JPL, MISR Team)

ESTUARY: THE LOWER HEATER

In Chinese medicine, the estuary region would correspond to the lower heater—the abdominal territory below our navels, encompassing our kidneys, bladder, large intestine, uterus, and genitals. Not surprisingly, the genital portion fell squarely in New York harbor; if the Hudson Valley had genitals, they surely would be the part that creates the vibrant sexyopolis of New York City! The upper border of the lower heater is marked by the navel, which would make the Peekskill Bay a sort of geographic belly button.

This idea made me giggle, as I immediately pictured a town called Big-Belly-Button-on-the-Hudson and the crazy kind of tourist attractions one could build there. But then my joke gave way to curiosity, as I recalled that many cultures describe their homelands as the center or navel of the world. The Greeks even had a word for it—*omphalos,* the world's navel. In Greek literature, Omphalos was widely represented as a holy mountain or island arising from the primeval waters of chaos. This seemed like a fitting description of the area right around Peekskill. Though it wasn't an island, the land did seem to rise out of the primeval waters of the Hudson. Of course, all places can't be the center of the world, and I didn't believe that Peekskill, New York, was actually the center of anything; but the perfect fit of symbolic imagery with the surrounding reality was powerful. Perhaps there are many navels of the world, all connecting to some deeper center.

MARSHLAND: THE MIDDLE HEATER

On our bodies, the middle heater exists between the navel and bottom of the breastbone, ending at a point just beneath the heart. The middle heater includes the liver, spleen, stomach, small intestine, and gallbladder—the main digestive organs. The Hudson's middle heater is marshland, which extends from Peekskill to Troy. Marshes form on lowlands that are regularly flooded during wet seasons and high tides. Nutrients that flow into marshy areas during flood times are stored in the plants, which in turn become food and shelter for birds, fish, and other creatures. The deep tidal river marshes of the Hudson Highlands are a rare type of ecosystem in the eastern United States, yet are key factors in the health of many significant species of East Coast wildlife, including bald eagles, striped bass, and the Atlantic sturgeon.

The way that marshland captures nutrients from tidewater and makes them available to other life-forms is similar to the process of digestion: our digestive organs capture—via breakdown—nutrients from the foods we ingest, then redistribute them to the rest of the body.

FORESTLAND: THE UPPER HEATER

Further upstream, the river's middle section meets the upper heater right around Troy, where the mighty Mohawk River joins the Hudson.

The upper region is designated forestland. The river is freshwater here, running pure from the Adirondack lake that is its source, above the reach of the tidal flows from the ocean. The water is clear and highly oxygenated. The Hudson's upper-heater forestland is characterized by spruce and fir forests. The river here is home to trout, northern pike, pickerel, sunfish, bass, and perch.

On our bodies, the junction of the middle and upper heaters is located just between our breasts—at the heart. In some ways, I could imagine this geographical spot as a cultural heart of the region: in the prerailroad age the confluence of two major rivers would have been a major center of activity; nowadays, it is the site of New York State's capital. In Chinese medicine, the upper heater houses the lungs as well as the heart. It wasn't much of a stretch to see the mountains and forests of this area as lungs: trees breathe, exchanging gases with the atmosphere just like our lungs. They even look like lungs, their many branches mirroring the branching reach of the lungs' alveoli.

If the Hudson was, in some way, a corollary of the Conception Vessel, what would that mean? The Conception Vessel is part of an unusual group of channels in Chinese medicine, known as the Extraordinary Vessels. They're extraordinary because they exist outside of the main network of twelve "regular" meridians that connect directly to the organs—like the Kidney meridian, the Heart meridian, the Spleen meridian, and so forth. Instead, the eight Extraordinary Vessels act as reservoirs of energy for the main channels. In ancient medical texts these vessels are often described as rivers that receive overflow energy from the main channels and can transfer it back when needed.

The Extraordinary (also called Extra) Vessels have a deeper significance as well: they form at conception, from a blend of our ancestral energies with the spark of new life that is unique to each individual. The Extra Vessels guide the subsequent growth and development of our bodies. Throughout our lives, they serve as powerful links to our deepest levels of being, connecting our present selves to the eternal energies we carry from generation to generation. Many modern acupuncturists liken these Extraordinary Vessels to our DNA.

The Conception Vessel is the first of these Extraordinary meridians to form within us. It is the first tendril of new life, which grows to become the midline of our bodies, running essentially from our genitals to the frenum depression just below the lower lip. Its companion, the Governing Vessel, marks the midline on the back of the body. From this essential circuit the other Extraordinary Vessels arise; together they create an energetic blueprint that guides the formation and functioning of the embryo, the development of the fetus, and the growth of the person born thereafter. Because of its progenitive relationship to the rest of our bodies, the Conception Vessel retains a large influence over our genital and reproductive systems, our organs, and our vital energy.

As one of the Extraordinary Vessels, the Conception Vessel accepts overflow from the regular vessels. Energy or blood that overwhelms the body's immediate needs can be stored in the Conception Vessel and returned to the regular vessels as needed. This overflow/storage function is very like the definitions of estuary and marshland described in the newspaper. However, in addition to receiving the overflow energies of the ocean, the Hudson had also become a major receptacle of the region's overflow energy from industry—it has been a dumping ground for industrial pollution for almost two hundred years, the radioactive waste from Indian Point being just the biggest example.

The Conception Vessel metaphor grew more interesting the more I thought about it. One of the most unusual details about the Conception Vessel in Chinese medicine is its origin: it is considered the first meridian to form in the developing embryo. While the Hudson certainly wasn't the first river to form in this part of the world, it was in many ways the river that conceived the character of the New World—in both its beauties and its miseries. Though he didn't know it when he sailed the *Half Moon* up the "Great River of the Mountains," as he called it, Henry Hudson forged a pathway that led to the conception of America.

In the span of a few short years, the Hudson Valley region, including Manhattan, became integral to the economic and cultural power of the New World. From the days of the Revolution onward, the area became a symbol of the nation's birth into independence and gave rise to the first truly American schools of art and literature, the Industrial age, the American military, and the environmental movement. But as industry expanded its demands into the twentieth century, the river valley also became a dark symbol of environmental destruction, cultural genocide, and the prioritization of profit for a few over the well-being of the many. As power-industry giants like Con Edison and General Electric took what they wanted from the Hudson, they left it so toxic that many species could no longer survive there. It became unsafe for humans to fish, or even swim, in the river.

As a child of this nation I grapple with its legacy: we are a country built on the wholesale destruction of the people and landscapes we displaced. When I think of Hudson's first journey—of the conception that led to this nation—I can't help but imagine an alternate reality. One in which the Europeans came in a spirit of peace and humility and built the economy with respect for the land and its people. What if the Europeans had willingly learned from the First People and had grown into a nation that lived in harmony with the living landscape? I can hardly even imagine it.

However, when I activate a client's Conception Vessel, I don't think to myself, "What if this person were different?" Instead I think of the Conception Vessel as empowering a person's potential: touching the best self that he or she has the possibility of becoming. I don't believe that I know who that person is or what she might become; I simply trust that she has a best self, and that her own body contains the power to become it.

Looking at history this way, I could believe that the Hudson contained the seed of this country's best possible self. I could also understand that this potential had become diseased—deformed by the heat of greed and corporate privilege, like the excess energy that can plague the Conception Vessel. I knew that the Indian Point nuclear power plant wasn't the cause of this underlying disease, but it was surely a symptom. And on those terms, it was something I could imagine treating.

If I wanted to "needle" this river and divert some of the excess heat and energy of Indian Point back into the regular channels, how would I do it? I looked through a few acupuncture texts and found this, translated from a second-century manual called the *Classic of Difficulties,* "When the Extraordinary meridians are under the attack of the vicious energy that blocks up circulation, it will give rise to swelling and hot sensations which should be treated by stone-needles."[1]

I gasped. *Stone needles?* Just what I had been planning to do! Intellectually, I knew that stone tools and needles were used to perform acupuncture before the widespread use of metal needles. From this perspective there was nothing unusual about the injunction to use stone. But on another level, this citation felt like proof that a stone circle would be a valid method of healing the river—as though a voice from two thousand years ago had reached through time to tell me my plan was a good one.

If the Hudson was the Conception Vessel, then Indian Point would be sitting right on the navel. In Oriental medicine, the navel is an extremely important part of the body, one of the three places where we can directly exchange life-force energy with the universe. (The others are through the breath and through the process of digestion.) Called the Spirit Gate or Spirit Palace, the navel is a gateway through which we access universal energy as well as the life-force energy that is stored within our kidneys. What might be the consequences, then, of having a nuclear power plant located right there?

On one hand, the navel seems an appropriate place for a power station. So much energy is housed behind the navel, this region is essentially the "power plant" of our bodies. We don't access that energy by needling the navel, though: instead we might gently blow smoke from burning herbs toward it. This technique is called *moxibustion* or *moxa.* In this sense, I could imagine Indian Point as a giant moxa pole, sending warmth into the body of the valley.

On the other hand, Indian Point's "smoke" is not gently burning herbs. It is hot, heavy, toxic smoke and superheated water, which puts an enormous toxic burden on all plant and animal life in the region. Indian Point regularly discharges water that is 95–100 degrees Fahrenheit,[2] which is beyond the lethal point for many species. And it never stops: an "attack of vicious energy," just like the *Classic of Difficulties* described.

In addition to the herbal smoke that is applied directly to the navel, the Conception Vessel—like the other Extraordinary Vessels—can be accessed via a special acupuncture point called its opening point. An acupuncture needle at the opening point readies the points on the meridian for further activity, which might include more acupuncture, moxibustion, essential oils, or massage.

For the Conception Vessel, the opening point is located on both wrists at a point named *Lie Que*—"Broken Sequence." If I truly believed that the Hudson River corresponded to the Conception Vessel in some essential way, I would need to find the Lie Que point. At the moment, this seemed like a difficult and overly specific task. How would I distinguish this one particular point in the entirety of the landscape? As I had done with other confusing questions about this project, I just let this one go. If I couldn't figure it out now, I was not going to persist; I would just keep moving forward.

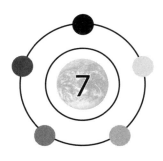

Divided Waters

I began to wonder what the next step of my project would be. In the back of my mind I had been rolling over the names Venerable Dhyani had given me to consult in the building of a stone circle: Ivan McBeth and Patrick MacManaway. At this stage I couldn't imagine what I might consult them about; I had no plan yet. I did, however, have a lot of enthusiasm and momentum—new ideas and possibilities came to me almost every day—and I wasn't ready to give up that creative engagement to some expert, no matter how highly recommended.

Still, it seemed like a good idea to begin to find out about these people. I had heard Ivan McBeth's name somewhere before. He'd been described as "a guy who builds stone circles." An unusual occupation, but it sure fit my needs. An Internet search furnished a few more details, connecting Ivan to some geomancers and dowsers whose names sounded vaguely familiar to me.

Elsewhere around the web, Ivan was described as a Druid and a wizard and a builder of stone circles. He identified with the ancient Celtic earth magic that had shaped his British homeland, conversing with fairies and Little People, celebrating the solstices and equinoxes, as well as the cross-quarter holidays—Samhain, Imbolc, Lughnasa, and Beltane. I knew a little bit about Celtic traditions, though I hadn't known that there were any modern Druids. I liked the fact that Ivan unabashedly associated himself with ancient magic and joyfully reclaimed old traditions—like stone circle building—for the modern world.

Ivan had also written a book, *The Crystal Journey*,[1] which could be downloaded directly to my computer. I began to read it that same evening and discovered that Ivan was a clear and inspired writer, and that his metaphysical adventure was a gripping story. Describing his experiences in India, the Himalayas, and rural Britain, Ivan laid out details of how he learned to communicate with beings as diverse as stones, snakes, water, and crystals. He was genuine and openhearted, and I knew as I sat glued to my computer screen that I'd be lucky to have his input on my project.

Hours later, I emerged from his tale of spiritual discovery with a palpable sense of excitement. Particularly fascinating to me were Ivan's stories about crystals: they literally spoke to him. And sang to him, from the depths where they lay buried, so that he heard music and dug up beautiful crystals seemingly everywhere he went.

Even more intriguing was the fact that Ivan gave crystals back to the earth. He *planted* them with care and intention—the way the rest of us plant seeds—whenever he wanted to offer something to the land. Ivan wrote that he thought of these crystals as seeds of healing and pictured them connecting to each other all around the globe in a single kinetic web. He even mapped the web, marking places in the world where he, or someone he knew, had planted a quartz crystal.

This was acupuncture. As soon as I read Ivan's descriptions of planting crystals, I pictured myself doing the same thing. Crystals are a lot like needles. Their clean lines and pointed tips give them the ability to focus energy, rather like a laser. But whereas lasers will beam focused energy from electric current, crystals and acupuncture needles don't have an external source of power—they focus the energy around them.

I thought about the bags of small quartz crystals I had dug up years before on an idyllic road trip to Arkansas with my good friends Patsy and Stacey. Digging for those crystals had been an otherworldly experience. The days were bright and hot, and the sun shivered in the air with a light so focused it fairly hummed. My body felt like it was vibrating. In retrospect, I believe it was the crystals in the ground that were vibrating; my body was attuning to them. At the end of each day, my friends and I would wash our crystals in the shallows of a big lake. As the quartz rocked gently in the water, the evening sunlight glanced off dozens of crystalline facets, creating a shimmering fairy dance of light. At night we dreamed of crystals, their pristine geometry filling our minds in place of words or more familiar forms. We woke up peaceful and full of wonder at these strange dreams and decided among ourselves that shape itself must be a language, spoken by crystalline beings.

Since that journey seven years before, my crystals had moved with me from house to house. I looked at them from time to time but hadn't known what to do with them until this moment. Now I knew I could reimagine them as acupuncture needles and plant them in the ground around Indian Point.

The next day I called James and told him about crystal needles. He was as excited as I was, and we quickly made a plan to meet as soon as we could—the following week—to plant some. In the meantime, I decided to write to Ivan. I didn't yet know what I wanted him to do, but I trusted that those details would emerge later.

I sent Ivan an e-mail introducing myself and the idea of a stone circle. I didn't want to speak directly about the Indian Point nuclear power plant in an e-mail, because I had heard that certain key words in e-mails and telephone conversations would trigger scrutiny from national security watchdogs. Since my car had already been showing up regularly within full view of the security cameras all around Indian Point, I didn't want to create any more red flags. I wrote to Ivan about a place where "electricity is generated in an unhealthy way" and hoped that he wouldn't find me too paranoid.

Was I being too paranoid? Hard to tell. This was post–9/11 America, and terrorism was a very real concern. Just a few months before, I had met a man at a party who told me a story of stopping his car one morning on his way to work to take a picture of a beautiful view by a bridge over the

Hudson. As he knelt on the ground to frame the picture in his viewfinder, he heard two cars screeching to a halt nearby. The next thing he heard was automatic rifles being cocked next to his head and voices shouting at him to drop the camera. This man spent two hours being questioned at a police station before they decided to let him go. They kept his camera.

I didn't want any run-ins with the police, so I expended some effort to keep myself under the radar. I wrote to Ivan in coded terms, and he was perceptive enough to be similarly guarded when he wrote back. He said that he was interested in helping with my stone circle project and would like to meet with me to get a sense of the region and the problems the river was facing. He agreed that standing stones can act like huge acupuncture needles that profoundly affect the life force of the Earth. "I believe that the Earth gives instructions to those with ears to hear," he wrote, "whenever she wants her energy body to be tweaked into new configurations. In fact, it seems to be the case that once certain acupuncturists have been trained to work on the human body, they are then recruited by the Earth." He personally knew of several such people and suspected that there were many more.

Wow, he really gets it, I thought to myself as I read Ivan's words. He had been doing land-healing work for years already and considered it normal. Moreover, he easily understood my plans to create an acupuncture treatment for the river and had even met others like me who had done similar things! I felt like I had stumbled through the looking glass, into a world where I really fit in. It was a good—though unusual—feeling.

Ivan mentioned that he would be visiting the northeastern United States in May and June and could perhaps visit me for a few days in early June to explore the land with me. I eagerly wrote back and thanked him, and we agreed to put the dates in our calendars. At the moment—in late March—I had no idea what I would do with Ivan when he got here. But June seemed a lifetime away, and I still had a lot of exploring to do. I trusted that by the time Ivan came, I would have some kind of a plan. In the meantime, I decided that my next step would be planting crystals at Jones Point.

We went in James's car this time, so that mine wouldn't be showing up too often on the security footage. Just as before, we could feel the energy of the air change as soon as we began our descent into the valley that held the small neighborhood of Jones Point. I noticed enormous tension in my stomach and couldn't take a deep enough breath to feel comfortable. I also had a faint headache across my forehead. James felt tension in the back of his head and described a sudden restlessness that made him want to jump out of the car and move around.

As we drove down the hill, James and I tried to make sense of that tension in our bodies. If we were just making it up, these symptoms would not appear the same way at this exact place every time. We had to be feeling something real, though we had no words to describe that something except to call it *energy*. I dislike the word, because it sounds so vague and New Agey, but I needed some way to describe the invisible and intangible yuckiness that pervaded this area. A miasm? A pall? Evil Qi? The vapors? Whatever we chose to call it, it was bad energy.

We parked the car and hopped out to explore the Pentecostal church that stood sentinel at the entrance to Jones Point. The doors were locked, and there was no one around, although two white vans sat parked out front. For some reason, those unmarked vans gave me the creeps; they were so featureless that they looked designed to be unnoticed—like vehicles for a crime gang or government operatives. The church's sign held an apocalyptic message about the devil, which added to the sinister feel of the place. I badly wanted to get away. The nuclear power plant loomed from across the river.

Without thinking about it, I rushed toward a triangle of sparse woods beside the church. It was the least creepy place around and seemed to offer a thin protection from the heavy air. But even standing next to the trees, I couldn't escape the clenching of my stomach or the dragging on my nerves. I wanted to howl.

"My diaphragm's getting tighter and tighter," said James. "Maybe we should put in a few needles." With a start I remembered that we had come here with a purpose; I pulled a bag of crystals from my coat

pocket and chose one, about an inch long and the width of my pin-
kie finger. James began poking around on the ground, finding a place
by a small sapling where he dug a hole through the snow and into the
ground. I circled my hand around the crystal and said a short prayer,
hoping that the ground would accept this healing seed and let it grow,
until the landscape could receive exactly the healing it needed. I pressed
the quartz into the ground, point down, and covered it over with dirt.
As James sprinkled cornmeal over the newly buried crystal I felt a shift.
Not one of those time gaps where everything merges together, but something more immediate, like the *click* and *whirr* of tumblers falling in a
lock. Something had *moved*.

Was I imagining that small shift inside me? Didn't my breath come
easier now? The tight wire around my stomach was surely a bit looser.
Yes, it was unmistakable. I laughed out loud. James at the same time
said "Hah. It's different!" We looked at each other, smiling. My mind
reeled with the truth of it: one tiny crystal. Oh, the possibilities.

"What point did we just needle?" James asked. According to the map
from the Hudson River Museum, Jones Point was just above the dividing
point between the lower heater/estuary part of the river and the middle
heater/marshland part. On a body, this point is just above the navel. It is
known as Conception Vessel 9 and Divided Waters. "Where the waters
divide," I murmured—between estuary and marshland. Could we have
imagined a more appropriate name? I silently offered James the bag of
crystals and he pulled out two. "Let's do a few more," he said.

We ran around the block of trees and planted crystals in each
cardinal direction, then one in the middle. With each crystal, I felt a
subtle shift inside my body as imperceptible cells altered in just-barely-
perceptible ways. I wished for a bright digital readout that could show
me exactly what was happening, but of course there would be no such
thing. We had to read our instincts instead, and trust them.

James and I walked across the street to the railroad tracks that ran
along the river's edge. Nothing standing between us and the power
plant now, just the wide still bay endlessly recirculating god only knows

what onto this shore. We planted a string of crystals alongside the track, envisioning a web of scintillating light catching any unhealthy atoms and transforming them into their purest counterparts.

After an hour or so in that landscape I needed to leave. My stomach felt better but still not right, and I wanted to breathe good air again. James and I walked slowly back to the car, taking deep breaths, and marveling at the difference from when we had arrived. The miasmic pall was still there, but ever so slightly lessened. I wondered what it would take to make a real and lasting change here. Our crystals were so small, I couldn't imagine that they would be enough to do the trick, even if we planted hundreds of them. But giant boulders? A circle of stones? Maybe, just maybe.

That night, I was exhausted but exhilarated. James and I had done something really new—we had given acupuncture to the Earth—and it had felt effective, albeit in a small way. Surely we were not the first to have discovered this—Ivan had written of others who have found ways to acupuncture the planet. I turned to my computer, but an Internet search for *earth acupuncture* turned up only general metaphors: how dance was like acupuncture for the Earth, how ley lines were like meridians. Some deeper digging turned up an out-of-print book from the 1970s called *Needles of Stone*.[2] The author, Tom Graves, had been studying the earthworks and stone circles that dot Great Britain, many of them built centuries or possibly millennia ago. Graves proposed that Britain's megalithic stone circles were a form of geomancy—of acupuncture, essentially—that was performed along the ley lines.

According to Graves, these stone circles were "like acupuncture" but were not true acupuncture, because there was no meridian system or tradition of acupuncture for the landscape. He discovered through his research that China hadn't really developed a megalithic culture like the one that produced the British standing stones and henges. China had developed feng shui—a system of analyzing and modifying the flow of energy in the landscape—but its modifications were ones that altered existing hills and rivers, rather than inserting "needles" at specific points. "But if we scale up another Chinese system," Graves wrote, "—acupuncture—to landscape dimensions, and combine it with feng shui, we would have a system of geomancy that closely resembles what we can see of the megalithic geomancy in Britain. In a system of earth-acupuncture, there could hardly be a more obvious 'needle' than a standing stone."[3]

I realized with pride that this "scaling up" of acupuncture was exactly what I had been doing: locating pulse points at three, six, and nine miles, identifying the Hudson as the Conception Vessel—these practices met Graves's conditions for true Earth acupuncture. This made me very happy; I was glad that other people were thinking about healing the Earth in the same way that I was thinking about it. It also helped me to understand why the crystal needles we had planted that day had felt somewhat effective, but not powerful like an acupuncture treatment. Our plantings had been kind of random; there was no system underlying the places we had chosen.

That was not scaled-up acupuncture, it was more like the "sham" acupuncture that medical studies sometimes use when they want to evaluate acupuncture's effectiveness. Sham acupuncture places acupuncture needles in locations that are not generally recognized as acupuncture points, the thought being that acupuncture in the wrong places would have no effect, allowing researchers to then discern the effects of "real" acupuncture in comparison. The problem with this approach, as professional acupuncturists often discuss, is that even fake acupuncture has some benefits. Evidently, the simple act of communicating with the body's energy grid is itself a form of medicine. Our bodies, like the Earth, flourish under our gaze; they heal in subtle ways *just by being acknowledged.*

What amazed me was that even this small-scale healing could have some effect. It showed me that I was not completely helpless in the face of the problems at Indian Point, and that I did not need to be a superhero to help the river heal. I could use the skills I already had, and the intention that had been instilled in me months ago by a clear vision, to plant a few small seeds of blessing. I fervently hoped they would grow.

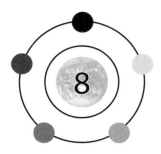

Thunder Mountain

I was excited about the crystals we had planted at Jones Point, but I knew that this was not the acupuncture treatment I had committed myself to giving the river. The planted crystals were more like a preliminary treatment—something like the palpation I do before I put needles into someone. The gentle, focused touch of palpation brings a client's awareness to signs that have previously registered only as problems.

The palpation at Jones Point had showed us that the landscape would respond to our work: we had clearly felt changes with each crystal needle. The next point I wanted to palpate was Dunderberg Mountain, which loomed up behind Jones Point on the western side of the river. The first time James and I had tried to climb it, we had been unable to find the trailhead. I wanted to try again, however, so James and I made a plan to go the following weekend.

Our chosen day proved rainy and dark, however, and a bad day for hiking a steep trail even if we could find it. James suggested that I meet him and Laura for lunch instead, and we could talk about our next steps. At a diner on Peekskill's waterfront, Laura pulled out a folder of satellite pictures and old maps of the region that she and James had found on the Internet. The pictures showed the river and land around Indian Point, and we talked about the images while we ate.

The map appeared to date from the 1930s. It was hand drawn and detailed the recreation activities of the Palisades Interstate Park—primarily on Dunderberg and its neighbor, Bear Mountain. In a region dotted with iron mines, both Dunderberg and Bear Mountain were crisscrossed by hiking and ski trails, as well as refreshment stands. Bear Mountain had ski jumps, trail shelters, and campgrounds as well, while Dunderberg was webbed with a red trail that the map's legend identified as an abandoned spiral railway. Evidently an enterprising company had, at the height of the tourist boom in the late 1800s, tried to build a light-rail tourist train to the top of Dunderberg but had never completed the project.

Looking next at the satellite map, the three of us were struck by the sweeping turns the river took right near Indian Point (fig. 8.1). These

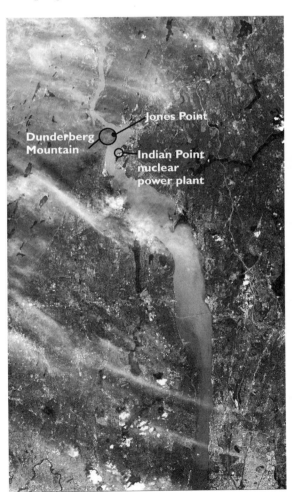

Fig. 8.1. Satellite view of the Hudson River showing the sharp turns in the river just above the power plant (photo by NASA/ GSFC/METI/ ERSDAC/JAROS, and U.S./Japan ASTER Science Team)

were the turns that made the water so slack between Indian Point and Jones Point. A fairly straight course ran both north and south of the area, but for a five-mile section, the river ricocheted around as though it had been stretched. We could clearly see that the eastern and western shores had once been joined together—like a jigsaw puzzle, there was a tab for every slot and a match for every edge of land. Somehow the land had split and the river had pushed its way up or through.

Laura joked that maybe Dunderberg had refused to move out of the way when the Hudson was laying its course, forcing the river into a big detour around the mountain's landmass. We all laughed, but the joke had a weird feeling of truth; once the idea had been spoken, we couldn't help but see that map as a story of the-mountain-that-wouldn't-move. If the land were somehow stronger than the river, the Hudson would indeed have built a course around it. This would explain the location of the turns in the river, as well as the feeling Dunderberg gave off of intransigent power.

We wondered about that power—why we felt it and where it came from—and we also admired it. Dunderberg was a force in the region in a way that the other mountains just weren't. Farther upriver Storm King and Breakneck were pretty dramatic, but down at this end of the Highlands, Dunderberg was clearly the boss. I also recognized that Dunderberg had been coming up more and more frequently in our conversations about Indian Point; perhaps the mountain had some yet to be discovered role in our stone circle project.

On the day that James and I had planned, for the third time, to hike up Dunderberg, I awoke to freezing rain and harsh wind. The weather was so nasty I hardly wanted to leave the house, let alone climb a mountain. "It's like the mountain doesn't want us to come," I thought to myself. But then, why should it want us? We were strangers and had made no overtures. People who respect the land ask permission for what they take and for what they use; perhaps we needed to ask permission even to use a trail. After all, a trail would lead to the mountain's inner world.

In Native American traditions, you talk to all kinds of beings—spirits, mountains, trees, ancestors, even insects—before attempting to engage with them on a physical plane. This basic act of acknowledgment sets the stage for any further interactions. Perhaps if James and I spoke to the mountain we could establish some kind of relationship, and Dunderberg might let us a little closer next time. We decided to each spend a little time during the next few weeks making prayers to Dunderberg and trying to present ourselves respectfully. James mentioned that he could actually see the mountain from the end of his driveway and could imagine sending greetings from there. "I'll just sort of wave hello and introduce myself," he said. "And maybe mention why we'd like to visit."

For my part I would call to the mountain during my meditation practice and try to explain our mission. Easier said than done. The next morning, as I came to the end of my meditation practice, I wasn't sure how to extend myself to Dunderberg. How do you call on a mountain from a dozen miles away? And how would a mountain hear?

I decided to create a mental picture of the mountain as I'd seen it from across the river, adding as many details as I could remember—the precise shape of its various slopes, the chain of dead trees like a hairline along the top ridge. I took a few moments to stabilize the image, to strengthen my sense of the mountain as a presence in its own right. Then I called out from my mind. "Mountain, do you recognize me?" I waited a minute, hoping I'd attracted its attention. "I'm the one who made you a promise," I said, and brought to my inner eye a picture of myself making a vow at the Hudson's edge. The scene came back to me: the dank smell of the shallows, the dusty feel of the cornmeal as it fell from my hands into dark water, my commitment to helping the river heal. Then I replayed the initial vision I'd had of river's wounds. "This is who I am," I said to the mountain, not knowing how else to make my case. "Will you let me come help?"

For the next few days I was consumed by an interest in Dunderberg, searching through books for mentions of the mountain. Most of the details came from the early days of the Dutch settlers, when the Hudson was the main transportation artery of the region. The unpredictable currents and dangerous conditions of sailing on the Hudson meant that a lot of stories were told about adventures and misadventures on the river. Dunderberg—which means "Thunder Mountain"—marked the southern gate of the section of river known as the Devil's Horse Race, or sometimes just the Race, well known for its narrow channel and perilous, often deadly, currents. In bad weather, northbound ships would lay anchor on the southern side of Dunderberg, often waiting days for the currents to calm before continuing on their journeys. One chronicler of Hudson lore described the mountain's role this way:

> It did not take many trips upriver to convince a sloop skipper that he should wait in the lee of Thunder Mountain [Dunderberg] if a west wind was blowing, because it would be dead ahead once he had rounded the point into the Race. When sloop commerce was at its height fifty sail might be waiting here, and when the wind changed or a flood tide came there would be a great fluttering of canvas as they came altogether around Jones Point. Then thunderous curses echoed in the gateway of the Highlands as the sloops veered into the swift deep water of the Race, taking the wind from each other, running athwart their rivals' bows, bumping and scraping. An hour later, having passed Anthony's Nose at the end of the Race, they would be a dignified peaceful parade of shining white sails more than a mile long, all well on their way toward the safe waters of Newburgh Bay.[1]

The dramatic landscape and weather of the Highlands also gave rise to fictional tales. Dutch sailors spoke in particular of a spirit of Dunderberg who controlled the weather, and who enjoyed creating fierce storms and winds. Washington Irving, the most famous of the Knickerbocker writers and the author of "The Legend of Sleepy Hollow," wrote about this spirit in his 1832 story called "The Storm-Ship."

The captains of the river craft talk of a little bulbous-bottomed Dutch goblin, in trunk hose and sugar-loafed hat, with a speaking-trumpet in his hand, which they say keeps about the Dunderberg. They declare that they have heard him, in stormy weather, in the midst of the turmoil, giving orders in Low Dutch for the piping up of a fresh gust of wind, or the rattling off of another thunder-clap.[2]

The goblin was said to torment ships and sailors all the way through the Highlands, until they had passed Pollopol's Island where, Irving wrote, "the jurisdiction of the Dunderberg potentate" ended.[3]

Reading these excerpts, I was glad to learn that my sense of Dunderberg's power had a historical precedent. The mountain was the gatekeeper of the Highlands: no wonder my thoughts kept returning there. With these delicious stories of Dunderberg in mind, James and I made our fourth plan to visit the mountain, on a day the following week when we were both free.

In the meantime, I was busy with my acupuncture practice and trying to figure out the next steps for my project. Whenever I treated a client's Conception Vessel during this time, I paid particular attention, looking for clues that might help me with my river project. I wanted to find a point near the river that corresponded to Lie Que, Lung 7—the Conception Vessel's opening point—which would theoretically help me to "open" the Hudson. One day I traced the Lung meridian on my arm, slowly moving my finger from Lung 1 and 2 on my chest to points 3, 4, and 5 on the inside of my upper arm. After Lung 6 near the wrist, the meridian makes a sharp turn outward to reach Lung 7 on the top of the wrist, before running back inward to the rest of the points (fig. 8.2). This configuration created a triangular detour on the meridian. As I went through those two sharp turns on my wrist I felt that they were somehow familiar, then startled to realize that the meridian had the same shape as the river around Dunderberg: the straightaway, the turn, and the second turn, before realigning along a straighter course. Where the mountain marked the pinpoint of the turn along the river, the bony

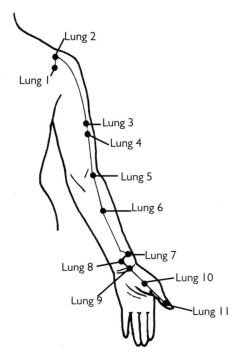

Fig. 8.2. Lung 7 on the Lung meridian mirrors the position
of Dunderberg Mountain on the bank of the Hudson.

point on my wrist was the turning point of the meridian, and the text-book location of Lung 7. A bony point—a mountain (fig. 8.3).

My heart began to beat a little faster. Could it be this easy? I went to my books and didn't know whether to laugh or cry at what I found there: "The qi of the Lung channel is gathered at Lung 6 . . . and from there *like a river breaking open a dam* the qi bursts forth and forks at Lung 7." Just like the Hudson breaking into the Devil's Horse Race at Dunderberg, the body's energy bursts out from Lung 7 and forks to other points. And then: "Ma Dan Yang describes Lung 7 as a 'thunderhead spitting fire.' The name of the point, [Lie Que] is an ancient expression for lightning."[4] Thunderhead. Lightning. Thunder Hill. Dunderberg. They were one and the same. I had been looking for Lung 7, and here it was, exactly the place I'd been drawn to.

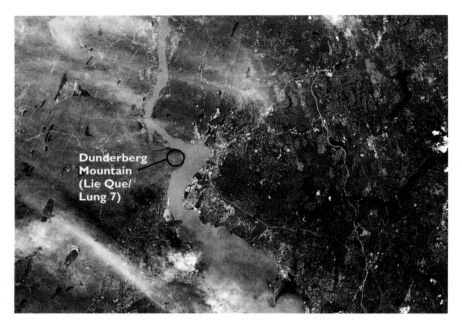

Fig. 8.3. Dunderberg as Lung 7 (photo by NASA/GSFC/METI/ERSDAC/JAROS, and U.S./Japan ASTER Science Team)

My knees were shaking as I sat down to think about this coincidence. How was it possible? These concordances of shape and name between the Hudson River and the Conception Vessel were powerful gifts that let me know I was on the right track, but they were also a puzzle. I'd thought I was making up my own story as I went along, arbitrarily deciding how to take pulses, what parts of the countryside were interesting, whether or not to assign a meridian to the Hudson. But these coincidences made it seem like someone else had written this story a long time ago. Instead of inventing a new way of working with the Earth, perhaps I was just rediscovering an old one: a beautiful tale of a landscape that answered to the map of a human body.

Humanity's oldest stories are just such tales; countless creation myths from around the world describe the Earth as a being—as a woman or a turtle or a child born of the Earth and sky. The Earth-being has relationships and adventures, is proactive and engaging; she has a story. I guess the Earth story for our troubled times is the tale of a planetary being who is ill and in desperate need of healing.

I decided to banish any lingering doubts I had about fulfilling my pledge to help heal the river and just embrace the fairy tale. The signs and portents might be leading me to nothing, but at this point the story itself had gotten so interesting that I needed to continue just to see where it would take me. Where I had once worried that I was in over my head, I now felt that I was exactly where I needed to be. My knowledge was the knowledge that was needed for this task, and my skills were the ones that would apply. The steps I needed to complete were unfolding before me, and I would continue to follow them until the treatment was done. Although I needed no further encouragement, I found that the earliest mentions of Lung 7 in ancient texts are found in a book called *Ode on the Obstructed River*.

   With a sigh, I realized that James and I had been unable to climb Dunderberg because we had had no idea of the mountain's true role in our story. Now that I saw it as Lie Que, the opening point of the Conception Vessel, all of the tales of its power made sense. I had been tuning in with the mountain every day for the past ten days or so, and now Dunderberg was beginning to show itself to me. I felt enormously grateful, and I sent a silent prayer of thanks to Dunderberg. I also reminded the mountain that James and I were coming to pay our respects in a few days. This time, I was sure we'd have no problem.

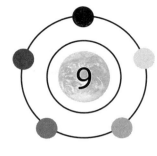

Dunderberg

The day we'd chosen to climb Dunderberg dawned bright and clear. "A good sign," I thought to myself. At least the goblin of Dunderberg didn't feel the need to call up another storm to keep us away. James and I arranged to meet in the small parking area at 8:30, with water and sandwiches in tow.

I put together a picnic lunch for myself, then set about assembling a small bundle with offerings for the mountain. Sage for smudging and some cornmeal to place on the ground, a typical way of "feeding" the mountain's spirit and, symbolically, the spirits of all beings who are hungry. But my mind hesitated today at the thought of cornmeal—it just didn't feel right. I remembered that even when I'd made my original vow to the river months ago, my cornmeal offering had felt a little out of place somehow, as though I were bringing someone a slightly inappropriate gift.

I could offer something else, but what? Sage leaves? I could crumble them and sprinkle them on the ground. That felt a little better, though still not quite right. I was rummaging through my supplies looking for dried sage when another possibility occurred to me: tobacco. This gift to the spirits, traditional in many Native cultures of the Americas, felt exactly right. Although I had been taught that tobacco's energies have become twisted by our worldwide misuse of it, I could today feel how well those energies still resonated with the local landscape. The Leni

Lenape, Delaware, and Wappinger peoples who had caretaken this area for so many centuries had surely offered tobacco in countless ceremonies and prayers. Something of the plant's ceremonial nature must still be intact, I reasoned. Thousands of years of sacred history are woven into the tobacco leaf's very DNA. Perhaps the mountain would be happy to have memories of those times stirred by our small gift.

Walking from the parking area, James and I easily found the white blaze that marked the beginning of the trail and marveled that we could have missed it the last time. I sprinkled a little tobacco to mark the spot, and we brushed ourselves with sage smoke to inaugurate our journey. A few yards in, we noticed a pair of maple saplings arching over our heads to form a natural gateway onto the trail. We paused before going through it, to make more offerings and prayers of greeting. The pungent smell of tobacco stung my nose as I sprinkled some leaves on the ground. "We're here!" I said to the mountain, "the ones who have been calling to you. Can we come in?" An unremarkable silence met us. We glanced at each other with excitement and walked through the gate.

The beginning of the trail was surprisingly open and flat, more like a field than a mountain. A mix of trees, vines, and prickly bushes dotted the landscape on either side. It was early spring, and the trees hadn't leafed yet, so our surroundings looked pretty bare. I found myself scanning eagerly for something interesting or beautiful to look at and was dismayed to find neither. "I guess the bad breath from Indian Point reaches this place, too," I remarked to James. "The land looks a little sickly." And it felt sickly too—peaceless and ugly.

After about fifteen minutes the trail floor finally gave onto rock and began to climb. Almost immediately I felt better—less disappointed and less apprehensive. Now rocks and briar bushes bordered the trail, and we scrambled up a cliff face too rocky in most places for trees to take root. Thin strips of trail linked to one another with small switchbacks that led us up a particularly steep stretch of mountainside. At one point I turned around and was startled to see the uncompromising bulk of the Indian Point nuclear power plant, larger and closer to me than it had ever been. My heart pounded and I felt afraid, as though it was poisoning everything around me. I rushed on, needing to get away, but was taken aback by a small tree standing right at the trail's next turn. Carved into the trunk of the tree at eye level were the letters *DNA*. I wondered who had carved it there, and why. Was it meant to be a warning of the power plant's effects?

We rounded a few more switchbacks, then climbed a rise. The right side of the trail was lined with boulders just a little taller than we were. My hand pushed against warm rock as I rose from a canyon into a clearing about twenty-five feet wide. The flat ground was a welcome respite after our steady ascent. We raced across the clearing to an edge that looked over the river, and over the power plant squatting below us. It was noticeably shortened by the angle of our view, and I felt somewhat less frightened. The simple fact of looking down on the plant instead of being dwarfed by it helped me feel more capable. I stared at the two matching concrete domes and wondered if I were looking into the power plant's eyes—the eyes of my adversary. "So this is what it feels like to meet a monster," I said, watching a plume of steam rise from somewhere.

"Our dragon," James added, "breathing fire and everything." We explored the far end of the clearing and found that it connected to another small clearing—equally round and almost the same size as the first—although shrouded by trees on the river side so we couldn't see the view. I liked the way the two clearings formed an infinity symbol, or a double helix as James saw it. The area felt open yet protected and full of promise. I wondered if a small stone circle could be built here, though it would have to be pretty tiny to fit. It would be no Stonehenge, but perhaps Stonehenge wasn't what was needed.

Another forty-five minutes on the trail brought us to an even more impressive lookout. From this height, almost eleven hundred feet above sea level, we could see for miles—the shape of the land formations, mountains, and valleys, and the region's small towns. A long stretch of the Hudson uncurled below us, and we could see both its sharp turns and its straightaways in uncomplicated detail. From this viewpoint Moheakantuk looked perfect: an Ur-river, an archetype, or a mythical landscape; it was hard to believe that it was filled with poisons and pain.

I am so lucky to see this, I thought. *This kind of beauty feels like it should be the province of gods or angels.* James and I sat down on some flattish rocks, unready to speak for fear of breaking the spell of beauty that surrounded us. The sight was so perfect I scarcely knew how to contain it. Tears filled my eyes as I realized that this was the way the river wanted to be—peaceful and shining in beauty. Perhaps this was why Moheakantuk had reached out to me, and probably to others as well—to help bring back its sense of majesty.

After a while James remarked that we'd been overcome by loveliness—instead of fear. Indeed, though the power plant was certainly visible here, it was dwarfed by the hugeness of the landscape, instead of dominating everything. The plant looked almost harmless from this remove and, oddly, almost cute, nestled as it was on the banks of the river like a child's toy arising from the playroom floor. Surrounded by such huge beauty, I could almost see something noble in that plant. I could imagine the brave dreams of those men who'd wanted to reach far into the skies and deep into the dark interior of our Earth, to tap the surging furnace of our planet and release the power of creation.

"And if that plant could generate megawatts of power without harming or even threatening anyone, it would be a thing of beauty," I said. "The accompanying destruction is really the problem." James said he was trying to picture a row of giant wind turbines on that point of land instead, or even water turbines beneath the surface of the churning river. Those would be less dangerous, we decided, but still models of hubris. Something about the ambition to generate power is, in its pure form, kind of poignant, even though the reality those ambitions have created is fraught with misery and danger. The desire for continuous energy is like our vaunting spirits, reaching past our limitations, yearning to be more like gods. A crazy endeavor? Yes, but not an incomprehensible one.

Any way you do it, though, siphoning power from the Earth is a bold move—an attempt to steal for humanity the powers of gods. Prometheus was doomed to spend eternity having his liver plucked out by vultures for having embarked on such a venture: why did our civilization's similar misdeeds go unpunished?

James and I continued to chat as we ate our lunches. We talked about the ways that this project kept dipping us into myths and fairy tales: there was something larger than life about it. "I guess the basic fact of a power plant on a river is inherently mythic," James suggested. "It brings us into relationship with the elements—with water and fire."

By the time James and I started back down the mountain, we were able to articulate the shift in our attitudes. We didn't hate the power plant anymore, we just wanted to help it change, so that its relationship with the surrounding land and people was more mutually beneficial. At this point, it was a relief to feel something like tenderness for the plant and its creators, instead of just burning anger.

As we neared the small round clearings, James and I both felt drawn to explore them again. In the first clearing, I had an unaccountable urge to lie down with my ear to the ground. "I just need to listen for a minute," I told James, and stretched out along the earth, brushing stones and leaves away from a small patch of dry dirt at my head. Ear down, as though listening for the vibration of an approaching train, I smelled the earth, decaying leaves, and the sweetness of the spring green that was about to burst upon us.

I closed my eyes, and wondered if I'd be able to discern a pulse beat here. Only my own heart and the sound of wind in the trees. An image formed in my mind—a brown and pregnant belly, stretched tight and beginning to labor. Who was this? I looked for a face but saw only the belly, a taut brown mountain, and felt the urgency of approaching birth.

"How strange," I said to James as I sat up and described my vision. "Without a face it seems more like a metaphorical birth than a physical one—like the Earth itself was giving birth to something, but to what?"

"Something new, I hope," James replied. "Maybe a new species or a new consciousness." I didn't quite get it. As we rose to continue our hike down the mountain, I was absorbed in that brownness. Hints of pain and of potential. What new idea needed to be conceived in order to eventuate this new birth? A poem I once read had described the Earth, in verse after verse, as "my beautiful nut-brown mother." These words matched my image exactly. My beautiful nut-brown mother—that was whose belly I'd seen. But who or what was she giving birth to? And what was I supposed to make of this image?

Simple word association led my thoughts to Nut, the Egyptian goddess of the sky. She stretches across from horizon to horizon and is said to give birth to the stars and planets every night. The ancient Egyptians built tall towers—obelisks—to represent the penis of the earth god, Geb. He would lie on the ground, penis reaching to the sky as he united himself with Nut and they together conceived the myriad forms of the heavens and earth.

I was back in the realm of mythology again, contemplating the familiar notion of the earth uniting with the sky. In many traditions, like the Egyptian one, this union is an act of conception that gives birth to the beings of the earth. Greek tales of Uranus and Gaia, Native American stories of Mother Earth and Father Sky, and countless others echoed this same imagery.

On the other hand, some stories—like the Judeo-Christian book of Genesis, and the Big Bang, and Taoist cosmology—emphasize that the domains of earth and the sky are a secondary stage in the development of creation; these traditions begin with an unsundered whole—a singularity, the Word, the Tao—that then splits into pieces. Many of these origin stories also have a correlate: a mystical tradition that suggests that the job of humankind is to make creation whole again—to maintain equilibrium among the fragmented parts, or even to bring them back together. These are mystical endeavors by nature, because they suggest that human beings have a purpose and that the purpose includes awareness of, and attention to, a greater order.

In reality, many religions and cultural traditions blend these views of creation together, describing a primordial chaos that splits into two or many, then the reunion of earth and sky, followed by a repopulation and refragmentation stage. Some religions have codified these ebbs and flows into lengthy ages that succeed each other to create a series of cycles: the thirteen baktuns of the Mayan calendar (5000-plus years); the long cycle of the Hindu calendar (432,000 years); the first, second, third, and fourth worlds of Hopi cosmology; and the long cycle of the Chinese calendar (60,000 years) are only some examples of these. Western astronomy has a scientific version of the great ages, too: the slow precession of the equinoxes, which track the Earth's predictable wobble on its axis through a 26,000-year cycle.

In every case, the core human mystical experience seems to involve our grappling with these basic facts of our existence: the earth beneath our feet, the sky above our heads, and our wee selves in between. How do we keep this thing running?

As we rounded the small switchbacks on our way back down the mountain, I nodded toward the power plant. The DNA letters carved into the tree now seemed like a caption for the picture. "Maybe the fact that it looks like a large penis is not exactly random," I said to James. "Maybe the plant has a constructive role to play in this new birth."

"The river is the Conception Vessel, after all," James reminded me. "I guess conception is what it's all about."

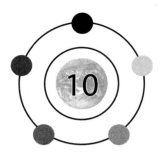

The Furies

I was elated after our first climb on Dunderberg. I felt that we had made contact with some elemental spirit of the mountain, that our respectful approach—which had evolved over the course of weeks and months—had gained for us a genuine audience with the king. From a blip on the map to a presence whose attention I had deliberately cultivated, Dunderberg now felt like the physical and psychological center of my project; I was pretty certain that it would be the site of our stone circle.

"I think the mountain holds the energy of what this place used to be," I said to James, one afternoon. Suddenly my heart sped up and my thoughts began to tumble; I was beginning to understand something. Concentrating hard in order to pull out the thread of words that would articulate the ideas flooding my mind, I spoke carefully. "I think that whatever power Dunderberg holds will turn out to be an exact antidote to the dark tyranny of Indian Point." As I spoke the words I felt something fall into place inside me.

"It's the fairy tale again!" James added with excitement. "The good giant has been put to sleep by a spell from the bad sorcerer, and it's our job to wake him up so he can free the kingdom." I nodded thoughtfully. Though the fairy tale was only a metaphor, it fit perfectly, helping to clarify the task ahead and our roles within it. Indian Point was like an evil sorcerer who terrorized the creatures all around it, and whose actual powers of destruction extended far beyond its physical boundaries.

Dunderberg was a sleeping giant who knew the secrets of a peaceful life but was surrounded by darkness and unable to communicate with the outside world. His beneficent powers needed to be rekindled. As for James and me, we didn't need to fight Indian Point or save the river through some series of heroic deeds, we simply needed to nourish the forces that belonged there—the awesome beauty of a mountain beside the water, the power of a healthy ecosystem, the primal strength of the natural world. Once the land was reconnected to its power, conditions around it would inevitably change.

This fairy tale freed us to work as healers instead of fighters, as we do in our acupuncture practices. We don't save or fix people; we just support their healthy parts and allow their natural wisdom to reassert itself. "But if we do succeed in waking the mountain," James said, pausing for a moment, "what do you think will happen?"

This was a good question. In healing work, we can rarely predict exactly how an individual's healing will transpire, and sometimes it's messy. Every now and then a client just gets steadily better, but more often than not—and especially with chronic conditions—there's some upheaval that comes first. Symptoms might get worse before they get better, or a new short-term illness appears, or someone goes through a personal crisis. These hardships are not signs of treatment failure; on the contrary, they are evidence that the body is reorganizing itself on a deep level. I like to call this the *snowshaker syndrome,* comparing the body to a snow globe. When you shake it up it looks like all hell is breaking loose, but the underlying structure is solid and the snow resettles onto it—beautifully—in a new pattern. In complementary medicine circles this phenomenon is often called a healing crisis.

In theory, a shake-up might be what the Hudson Valley needed in order to cast off the toxins of Indian Point and resettle itself into some healthier position. However, a nuclear power plant that sits on an earthquake fault would make any significant shake-up truly dangerous. Instead, we wanted the mountain to wake up slowly and peaceably, and for any shifts in the region to be gradual ones. We'd have to work slowly and carefully to ensure that the landscape had time to integrate any changes.

"Do you think Dunderberg Mountain is a he-giant or a she-giant?" James asked, changing the subject. The question made me uncomfortable. I felt that the answer should be obvious to me, but it wasn't. Intellectually, I expected the mountain to be feminine; after all, the earth was feminine and the mountain was a part of it. Sacred feminine energy also seemed like the logical force to counter the overbearing and very masculine energy of Indian Point. The problem was the mountain didn't *feel* feminine to me. It had a dark and brooding nature and kind of a violent temper, which we'd seen in the early literature about it and in our own experience. Of course there are aspects of the feminine that are dark and violent; I thought of Kali, the destroyer goddess of the Hindu pantheon, and Pele, the raging goddess of Hawaii's volcanoes. They both have archetypal tempers and legendary appetites for vengeance. In ancient Greece, the (female) Furies punished criminals with hideous torment. But Dunderberg's temper didn't feel like a fury. It felt . . . territorial.

"It's either masculine or some aspect of the feminine I've never considered before," I answered James. "I guess it's possible that the mountain may embody some energy that is more primal than the masculine/feminine divide." An earlier unsundered whole, like the Tao, that just *is*. "That may be why we just keep calling it *the mountain*." We considered these possibilities for a while, then decided to put the question of the mountain's gender on hold. We didn't really need an answer; what was important was how the question itself got us deeply engaged with this particular landscape. We were plumbing the nuances of our experience with it, and that meant we were listening.

As momentum was building around our healing work with the river, a parallel buildup was occurring in the social and political sphere. A subcommittee of the Westchester County government had been appointed to investigate the possibility of shutting down Indian Point for good.

Although the plant was owned by an out-of-state corporation, and its operations were overseen by state and federal agencies, the fact that Indian Point sat on Westchester County land meant that the county could, under certain conditions, revoke or discontinue the plant's license to operate.

The county executive (the highest elected official in the county) had voiced his interest in closing Indian Point down, but there were powerful political forces that very much wanted to keep it open; namely, the plant's corporate owner, which poured tons of money into the area every year and pulled out even more. But there were other power companies and big businesses that rebelled on principle against the idea of a public outcry affecting their corporate rights to operate as they chose, and these were continually pressuring state and federal governments to keep the public policy business-friendly.

Still, a year and a half after 9/11, the possibility of terrorist attacks on power plants was a common topic of discussion, and the volume of public sentiment on the matter had been steadily increasing. Local close-Indian-Point groups were seeing a surge of public interest, and one particularly powerful ad campaign had brought the debate to millions of rail and subway riders throughout the New York metropolitan area. The ad pictured Indian Point at the bull's-eye of a target. The words read, "Governor Pataki, Get the Target off our Backs! Close Indian Point." Local officials were no doubt hearing from their constituents about this issue, and the county had responded by selecting a subcommittee and scheduling a public hearing where citizens would be able to voice their thoughts about the plant.

I decided to go to this hearing, expecting it to be like other close-Indian-Point demonstrations I'd been to from time to time—fifteen or twenty committed people, trying valiantly to make their voices heard. Generally I was frustrated by these demonstrations, which attracted little attention and accomplished even less. I wanted to go to this one, though, because people in power would be listening for once. True, it was just a small committee, but it would be making its recommendations to county officials who actually had the power to shut Indian Point down.

I was surprised when I stepped into a crowd of hundreds crammed into the foyer of the auditorium. There was still an hour to go before the scheduled hearing, but people had shown up early to put their names on a list to speak to the committee. I was thrilled that the issue had evidently gained enough traction to draw this many people, and for a long time I just moved through the packed room, looking at faces and enjoying the buzz of excitement.

Suddenly a shout went up, "Keep it open!" and many voices joined in to repeat these words as a chant: "Keep! It! Open!" I looked around in bewilderment. Thirty or forty people in the crowd were moving toward the center of the foyer, chanting and pumping their fists in the air. I thought the people were here to try to get the plant shut down; what was happening?

"Entergy brought them in," said a man next to me, referring to the company that owned the nuclear power plant at Indian Point. "We saw the buses unloading earlier. It's meant to be a counterdemonstration, to make it look like there's a lot of local support for the plant." Two men close to me were part of the effort. I couldn't take my eyes off them; they almost glowed with anger. In boots and jeans, they had probably just come off a shift. Their legs were planted in a wide and menacing stance, their faces were dark red and rigid with fury as they shouted. And those fists, punching the air with every beat; if they were swinging a little lower they could really hurt people. I realized I was frightened; that much anger could easily explode into violence. Somehow Entergy had persuaded its employees to climb into buses on a rainy weeknight to show up at this hearing and demonstrate. What had they been told? How far had they been given permission to go?

By this time the Shut-It-Down people had collected themselves and started chanting, too. The tension level in the packed anteroom climbed even higher. As fervently as I wanted that plant shut down, I could not join this shouting match. It would only inflame the tensions on both sides, creating deeper enmity. Anger like this could never lead to positive change; it could only create more anger.

Real healing would have to come about in a different way. It would need to defuse this anger and unite the local residents in fighting a corporate power that did not have any of their best interests at heart. I began to pray for people to realize that they had more in common than they had separating them. I looked at the shouting men and women and focused on their hearts, wishing comfort and calming thoughts would come to them. I imagined the collective anger as a red fog that shrouded the room, then envisioned it shifting and lightening, becoming a pink mist that embraced everybody in a field of compassion before transforming into the faintest wisp of cloud and drifting away.

I couldn't tell if my prayers were helping. People were still shouting, but at least I was not caught up in it. I began to look around for other calm people, thinking we might collect ourselves together and radiate a different sensibility. The commotion in the foyer eventually came to the attention of the politicians inside the auditorium, who finally allowed us all to enter and be seated. The physical activity of movement managed to convert a lot of the angry energy into something more useful, and by the time all the people were seated things were noticeably calmer, though not necessarily less hostile.

After brief introductions, people were invited to speak one at a time, following the list that had been made up earlier. I was relieved each time a shut-it-downer spoke succinctly and effectively and cringed at those whose emotions made their words sound desperate or flighty or endless. The keep-it-open folks were sprinkled in and spoke mainly about the good jobs they had and didn't want to lose, and about how everyone's energy bills and taxes would skyrocket if Indian Point were forced to close.

There was some truth to the taxes part. The town of Buchanan had been incorporated specifically to house the power plant, which had arranged a sweetheart deal with the state that kept residents' property taxes so low that they couldn't help but be grateful for the plant's presence—and fearful of losing it. The higher-energy-bills argument was less certain. Different analysts had—not surprisingly—come up with very different figures, and several had concluded that between other energy sources and the redirection of some government subsidies now benefitting Indian Point, Hudson Valley customers might end up paying about 2.4 cents more per kilowatt for their electricity if Indian Point was to shut down. Hardly enough to strike fear into anyone's heart, yet the mere threat of higher bills was trotted out again and again as a way to squelch debate about the plant's continued existence. It was a difficult argument to fight, even with good research.

I listened with a sagging heart as more than one Indian Point employee spoke guilelessly of the faith he had in his fellow workers to do their jobs well and handle any problems that came up. While this was a beautiful and sincere declaration of community, it was also eerily unsettling. Did these men not realize that good intentions were only a small part of the picture? It seemed glaringly obvious to me that a leaking fuel rod or containment tank—or a terrorist attack—would not be the fault of a single technician doing a bad job, or a failure of teamwork. Big problems happen when multiple failures in smaller systems add up, or after some overwhelming influence that nobody could have anticipated—like an earthquake or tsunami or a planned attack. But these men spoke with a sense of injury in their voices and were offended that anyone would doubt their competence.

This, I realized, was the heart of the matter for the plant employees. They felt personally attacked when anyone criticized the plant's operations. But for those of us who wanted the plant closed down, the individual employees were barely on the radar. Yes, we could point to one or two incidents of security guards found sleeping on the job, or electricians who had installed faulty wiring, but by and large the problems we worried about were the ones that arose from decades of corporate neglect, shortsightedness, and corner-cutting. Worn-out equipment, structural collapse, fraudulent inspections, insufficient backup procedures, and the list goes on.

Experience has shown us that a serious radiation leak cannot be contained by even the most well-meaning team of employees, or even an efficient government. Yet Indian Point's owners were cynically telling their employees that this was the issue: that their neighbors had no faith in them.

The arguments went on for a few hours, until the committee finally got everyone to go away by promising a second hearing in a month's time. I left the auditorium depressed and numb. I was sad for those employees, who seemed like good and honorable men. They wanted to work hard and care for their families and didn't want their jobs to disappear or their taxes to go up. All that was understandable, but I wondered how they could close their minds to the potential for catastrophe. A disaster like the one at Chernobyl or, much later, at Fukushima would make this densely populated New York suburb uninhabitable. An explosion or a full meltdown could jeopardize forty million lives.

We live in a culture of nuclear denial, however. Possibilities that can be made to appear statistically unlikely are completely ignored—as if they could never happen. Federal law mandates an evacuation plan, for instance, for a ten-mile radius around every nuclear power plant in the country, in case of emergency. Yet fifty miles is the generally accepted peak-danger zone for nuclear disasters—and fifty miles was the area that the Nuclear Regulatory Commission recommended Americans evacuate during the Fukushima disaster in 2011.[1] A fifty-mile radius around Indian Point would be nearly impossible to evacuate, however: the area includes New York City and more than twenty million people.[2] Even within the official ten-mile evacuation zone, however, the plans are sketchy. This is one of the most densely populated regions in the country, and the plan for moving all of those people out on the limited, already packed roadways is accomplished with a great deal of what can only be called logistical license. Schoolchildren and adults without cars are supposed to wait at designated bus stops. Bus drivers are expected to drive willingly toward the danger in order to pick up these patient passengers, and parents are expected to *not* rush toward their children, but to wait for them at another location. Roads are expected to remain passable for the time it would take for three hundred thousand displaced people to move . . . somewhere else.[3]

All this is to say that the plans for emergency seem pretty much a fantasy. Perhaps a lot of public safety issues are regulated that way—with a wing and a prayer—but in our changing world, this kind of denial seems ever harder to maintain. The unthinkable is quickly becoming recurrent and mostly beyond human control at this point. Not all of it is beyond our control, however: aging, substandard nuclear facilities are an avoidable hazard. Poorly secured nuclear waste is an addressable issue. Compared to the problems of stabilizing the global climate, shutting down a single problematic nuclear power plant is not that hard. We just need to focus.

Public activism shut down the Shoreham nuclear power plant on Long Island, the San Onofre plant in California, and others. In 2014, public support encouraged the state of Vermont to revoke the operating license of its single nuclear power plant, Vermont Yankee. This plant is a sister to the Indian Point nuclear power plant that boasts the same outdated design and the same parent company, Entergy Nuclear. While the estimated $1.24 billion price tag for decommissioning Vermont Yankee is steep, that cost will be borne (in theory) by the plant's owners, and not by the people of Vermont, New Hampshire, and Massachusetts.

"The impossible will take a little while," sings Billie Holiday. "The difficult I'll do right now."

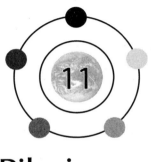

Pilgrimage

After the county hearings on Indian Point, I was depressed. Though I had been elated only days before, proud of the way I'd recognized Dunderberg Mountain as the genius loci of the region, I no longer saw how anything could combat the political and economic strength that Entergy wielded. The hearings had made clear how hard the corporate owners of Indian Point would fight to keep the plant open. They had a lot of money and a lot of strategists to help them tilt the public debate in their direction; they could outspend and outfox those who hoped for cleaner energy without even straining.

In contrast to these forces, my puny voice seemed inadequate, and my metaphysical efforts felt almost ridiculous. I didn't see how my work could make a whit of difference to the politicians or the frightened Entergy employees or the determined Entergy executives. Perhaps I needed to rethink my plans, or give up and move away. . . .

I drifted aimlessly through the next few weeks. I had lost faith in my project and had no enthusiasm for pursuing any more Indian Point adventures. I went to work and came home and mourned my helplessness. After a few weeks of my silence, James called to wonder where I'd been. When I told him about my low mood, he was not surprised—in fact he'd been depressed as well, though by different circumstances. In James's case, he'd learned that the financing for his new coffee shop was falling through. Feeling powerless to persuade the banking executives of the merits of his business plan, he grew angry and found his frustration exploding into his marriage. He reeled between depression and rage and felt that our relationship to the land and Dunderberg was pointless.

Discussing our separate stresses, James and I noticed that we both felt outmatched, faced with obstacles much larger than we were. We both had wondered in the past week whether we ought to give up—on the stone circle, on the coffee shop, on trying to make even a small difference in a giant world. James pointed out that we'd each come to a bump in the road—"or a mountain, I guess you could call it. And we need to decide for ourselves whether we're going to climb it, or turn around and forget it."

I thought of the actual mountain we had so recently climbed, and the weeks of preparation we had gone through to get there. Mountains are well-worn metaphors for difficult emotional terrain—clichés, really. But what if the mountain was more than just a metaphor? Maybe our journey to the mountain had engaged some deeper parts of ourselves that now needed attention. Like walking a labyrinth or a medicine wheel, perhaps the very act of climbing a mountain changes something inside of us.

In China and Tibet, some mountains are sacred. They are sites of holy pilgrimage that subtly alter the people who climb them. One of my favorite authors, Gretel Ehrlich, described mountain pilgrimages in her book *Questions of Heaven:* "For [Buddhist monks] pilgrimage wasn't only paying homage to a place of power, but also the transformation of the inner and outer environment through the physical act of walking, every step and breath altering the atmosphere, path and goal becoming the same."[1]

Poet and translator David Hinton explored similar terrain in his book *Hunger Mountain,* writing, "Wandering through this mountain's topography of forest and stream and rock, its weather and history, I'm wandering through myself in the form of a mountain that eludes me perfectly."[2] Ehrlich writes that the Chinese expression for "going on a pilgrimage"—*ch'ao-shan chin-hsiang*—translates directly as "'paying one's respects to the mountain,' as if the mountain were an empress or an ancestor before whom one must kneel."[3] Although Dunderberg is a tiny blip compared to the ten-thousand-foot slopes that attract Buddhist pilgrims around the world, perhaps its role in the Hudson River landscape was somehow similar.

While James and I had carefully paid our respects to Dunderberg, we had not considered what the journey might do to *us*. Now we were left with a kind of spiritual imbalance—the physical pilgrimage had been achieved, but our psychic transformations had been unrecognized and therefore incomplete. Viewed this way, the depressions we were each experiencing—and the circumstances that led to them—could help us complete this portion of our journeys. Any creative way of looking at the events that had discouraged us would help us change. We could meet adversity with hope, with wisdom, with determination, or firm decision—but we didn't need to slink away in defeat.

We decided that we would not fight our depressions, but go deeper into them. We each agreed to spend the next two weeks exploring our inner terrains to see what our landscapes were filled with. What fears and doubts, what angers, what questions, what core beliefs. This is how we would internalize the work we had begun and make the journey personal.

It was somewhat liberating—and scary—to give myself permission to explore my depths. Although I worried about what I might find there, I nevertheless made a list of all the things I could think of that were depressing me.

1. Indian Point
2. Trying to fight the system
3. The degradation of our world

Now what?

I looked at the list. All interrelated. All examples of decisions being made in places where ordinary individuals never have any influence. No wonder I was depressed; according to any kind of logic, nothing I did would make a difference. That's how depression leaches people of the desire to take action—when we feel useless, we make few attempts to change our situation because all efforts seem doomed from the outset. This lassitude pretty much guarantees that the situation will continue to oppress us, and we are caught in a destructive cycle of passivity and hopelessness.

And yet, positive changes do happen in the world—all the time. Sometimes protests do end wars or shutter destructive businesses. On Long Island and in New Hampshire successful protest movements had eventually led to the decommissioning of nuclear plants. Why couldn't it happen here? Or more to the point, what could I do to increase the possibility of its happening here?

In my life I have seen a great many people heal and change, in ways I wouldn't have foreseen. Surely a neighborhood, or a region, or a landscape could heal effectively as well, but what could be done to help such a healing come about? The people I had seen heal had all used tools—like acupuncture, psychotherapy, bodywork, prayer, and shamanic journeying. A variety of tools and an openness to discovering them seemed more important in each case than the specific tools that had been used. Such practices seemed able to rearrange some deeper thing.

When people are willing to engage their body, mind, and spirit without holding back or trying to control the outcome, shift happens at a quantum level. Somewhere deep inside, cells and molecules and tissues learn to completely reconfigure themselves, leading to exciting changes at all levels of being. I had seen diseases like cancer and lupus go away, lonely people find mates and get married, and unhappy wage earners discover their life's passion and blossom. I myself had been through several such deep reconfigurations—moving from chronic pain to painless well-being, from spiritual starvation to fulfillment, from work that destroyed me to work that made me whole. But I still wasn't done: for years I had been trying to find love, wondering where to find my partner, how to put myself in places where likely men might be. I had cultivated and practiced a deep love for the whole living world, yet had not met the man who would joyfully share his love with me. Years of loneliness had left me incredibly frustrated by my inability to *make it happen.* What did I have to do to get there?

This sounded an awful lot like what I was asking about Indian Point: What did I have to do to bring change? I knew that deep change was possible because I had been privileged to live it, assist it, and witness it more times than I could count. Now I needed to figure out how to ignite it—for myself as well as for the land. "But if I can't *make* change happen," I wondered to myself, "then how will it come?"

I thought about the deepest transformations I have seen. Alteration doesn't happen in a normal moment; it happens when we are at our very edge. Usually people hit some kind of bottom before change comes to them. They've had to give up everything they own, are living with uncountable loss. Often despair is what prompts someone to let go of whatever they'd been trying so hard to hang on to, but then the despair itself transforms—giving up becomes an act of liberation. Suddenly we are free from needing a particular thing to happen in a particular way. Whatever happens is okay in its own way.

So how could I bring myself to this edge of liberation? How could I let go of the things I so desperately wanted? I decided to imagine things turning out exactly the opposite of what I hoped for: *Maybe all my work is useless. Maybe the political system and economic infrastructure that drive Indian Point and its supporters is unshakable. Maybe the plant will never be shut down. Maybe I should stop devoting so much of my time and energy to this crazy and pointless endeavor.*

And then: *I have to admit that I may change nothing. I have to let it all go—my dream of helping the river, my dream of transmuting poison, my need to have something worthwhile to do with my time.*

So I decide to let go of my plans. Then I am left with . . . silence. No more clamor of possibilities. No more weighing of options. Just me observing the failure of my dreams: I may not be able to do a thing about the river, I may never know what it is like to be deeply loved, I may never have children. I lived in these thoughts for a day or two, feeling strangely calm. Maybe I should let the whole project drop. Then I'd have the time to take an interesting class, maybe meet some new people. Failure isn't necessarily all bad; there might be some new opportunities ahead.

But slowly, other thoughts began to assert themselves, mainly this— *I am enjoying the work.* I loved being out on the land, deep in meditation. I loved finding Chinese medicine woven into the world around me. I loved the fact that I had made a promise and had been willing to push myself deep into uncharted territory in order to keep that promise. I had genuine enthusiasm for what I was doing and liked my life while this work was a part of it.

Hmm. I think I would keep doing this, even if I knew the work to be useless. More than likely, I wouldn't ever really know if the river was somehow benefiting from my work. I had no real way to measure. Given that, I would need some other reason if I chose to continue. *Because I am growing something new,* I heard myself say. This was reason enough to keep going. Odd as it sounded, I was growing relationships with the river and the mountain. Not human relationships, but real ones nonetheless, in which I offered myself and received gifts from the mountain and river in response: visions, insights, and ideas.

With these realizations, I decided I would keep going with the stone circle project—not because I believed a specific change would happen as a result, but because the process itself was a deeply creative and satisfying one. My partners (the river, the mountain, and James) and I were making some new kind of art or magic. And it was the most exciting thing I'd ever done.

With fresh enthusiasm and a focus on the pleasures of the experience, I invited James and Laura to explore some new territory with me: a vacant Capuchin monastery in Garrison, New York, which perched on the eastern shore of the Hudson. The land was prime Hudson Highlands real estate and had once been the private estate of Hamilton Fish, a governor of New York and later secretary of state under Ulysses Grant. Rumor had it that the land had once been considered as the location for the Dalai Lama's personal library and was now being purchased by a nonprofit organization that was planning to turn it into a meditation and retreat center.

With this kind of history, I imagined that the land would be beautiful, protected, and peaceful—and it was. As we walked away from the road toward the river, James, Laura, and I found ourselves stepping into a quiet woodland carpeted with purple and green periwinkle. There were no trails, so we just wandered around, separating and coming together at random intervals. We were all drawn in the direction of the river and eventually found ourselves on a spectacular mountain promontory overlooking the Hudson, hundreds of feet below. An enormous concrete block about four feet square gave the mountainside a curiously unfinished feeling; no doubt a welcoming St. Francis statue had once stood upon this pedestal, whose truncated reach was now totally devoid of holiness.

Soon I found myself pulled away from the river and into the woods. James and Laura wanted to stay and admire the view for a while, so I left them and walked around on my own. A tightness in my diaphragm that bordered on nausea became my trail guide; I followed it for a few minutes, turning left or right as my gut demanded, until I came to a peaceful glen where a circle of giant trees stood in majesty. Seven ancient maples and oaks, each hundreds of years old, seemed to be presiding over this part of the landscape. I stood in the center of the circle and spun around slowly, greeting each tree. Then I offered some cornmeal in the center of the circle. "Thank you, grandfathers and grandmothers, for the peace you help to maintain on this land and for the wisdom you share with all beings. May your visions of the future take hold in our hearts and minds, and may we find the means to make them real."

I moved to a cluster of rocks outside the circle of trees and sat down. I closed my eyes and tuned in with the landscape, asking if anything was needed here. Was this site meant to have a stone circle on it, too? In a quick meditation, I tried to see this area from the point of view of the giant trees. They had seen so many creatures and habitats come and go over the centuries, perhaps they didn't even react to changes anymore.

What I saw in my mind's eye was that their territory was shrinking; the area of landscape that had once been the purview of this council of elders had been getting steadily smaller over time. The nearby roads and houses were not a problem; it was the machinery of heavy industry—and its pollutants—that disrupted the natural rhythms of the forest. I felt a small tick of hopelessness inside me, because there was nothing I could do about industrial pollution. Then I remembered that that wasn't my job; I just needed to support the trees. So I sent them more prayers of love and thanks and envisioned a primeval forest that was undisturbed by humankind. Then I saw a line of monks file quietly into the wood, where they stood in a circle and prayed. Clearly, these particular human beings were not disruptive to the landscape; on the contrary, they contributed their community and their strength to its well-being.

I opened my eyes to the warm sunshine and spent a few minutes just taking it all in. I knew that community was a fundamental principle of the Capuchins, who followed the teachings of St. Francis. I supposed that the circle of trees must have seemed a great symbol of prayer and community to the friars who first built this monastery in 1929. Even then, these trees would have been impressive. A trace of movement caught my attention and interrupted my train of thought. I saw a tiny black bug crawling across the back of my hand. I smiled at it and said hello to my fellow creature, feeling a strong sense of peace and even community toward it. As I watched, the bug's funny, crablike crawl gave me pause, and it occurred to me that this might be a tick.

I counted legs and found eight—an arachnid—instead of the six legs of the insect kingdom: a tick. I stared at it for a few seconds, feeling a confusion develop in my mind. I felt love for this tiny animal—it was part of creation and wondrous for that reason—but I knew that ticks can be dangerous. I didn't want to be ruled by fear, so I just brushed the tick off, trying to be gentle. "Even ticks deserve to be loved," I thought. I was proud of myself for remaining open and compassionate even with a tick on my hand. When I noticed a few more ticks crawling up my arm, I brushed them off as well and scolded them a little bit. "Now, now," I told them. "This is my arm, and you don't belong here." I would later have cause to regret this soft discipline, but it felt like enlightened behavior at the time.

I ran back for James and Laura and drew them to the circle of trees. As if following the same set of instructions, they each walked around the inside of the circle, touching the massive trunks and looking skyward. Then they each leaned their back against one of the giants and closed their eyes. For a moment I saw my friends as tree-beings themselves, joining in the council that was assembled here.

This circle of standing trees in a shady glade was both like and unlike the circle of standing stones I had envisioned for the outcropping on Dunderberg Mountain. Whereas this place felt protected and internal, its columned tree trunks drew my eyes upward to the sky; Dunderberg, on the other hand, felt raw and exposed, but its naked promontory drew the gaze downward, to the river. The two sites were yin and yang complements, perhaps—together describing something whole.

I couldn't imagine building any kind of stone circle here; none was needed. But nevertheless I felt that this site was also important to my greater goal of helping Moheakantuk to heal. I decided that when Ivan McBeth came in a few weeks to talk about building the stone circle, I would bring him here, as well as to Dunderberg. Maybe he would have a sense of how—or if—the council of trees should be a part of our work.

✦ Connecting with a Larger Landscape and Finding Its Pulse Points

After you have established connection with a tree, you can begin to explore more expansive territories. For this exercise, you can pick a homeowner's property, a pond or small lake, a park, a stream, or the like. Later, you can choose a much larger area like a mountain or river, but in the beginning you will have clearer results with a medium-sized territory.

1. Begin by looking at maps of your selected area. Road maps, hiking maps, and satellite images all provide different kinds of information, and each can help you deepen your understanding of your landscape. Look for roads and watercourses that run to and through it, and look around the edges of the property to see how the land connects to its surroundings. Even if you know the area well, map work is a great way to freshen your perspective.

2. With a map or satellite image in front of you, do a short meditation. Reach out to the landscape with your heart and mind and explain that you want to learn from it. Affirm your good intentions and your desire to visit in person.

3. Approach your selected area with respect. As you near the property line or boundary edge, pause and make an offering of nuts or cornmeal. If you are working with a body of water, stand on the bank or beach and sprinkle your offerings directly into the water. Remind the land who you are and that you are here to learn from it. Ask permission to enter.

4. Take a step back, and pay attention, looking for any signs of welcome or prohibition from the environment. An insect bite or sting, a rumble of thunder, or an aggressive bird or animal can all be responses suggesting that you leave. So can sensations of fear or foreboding. You will need to be honest about interpreting such signals and respectful in obeying them.

By the same token, overtly positive signals like a sudden burst of sunshine, butterflies, or birdsong, or sightings of wild animals are usually invitations. In Native American traditions, the specific kind of animal or bird carries great significance and often represents messages from the land about what it is offering and how you might best respond. Use reference books like *Animal-Speak* to help you understand these messages.*

If you don't perceive any signals at all from the landscape, it is all right to enter. Be aware, however, that you may have to work a little harder to establish a relationship in this case.

5. Enter your landscape, and walk around its edges. Use your eyes and ears to examine as much of the territory as you can, noticing variations in turf and vegetation as well as rock formations, tree stands, insects, and animal life. If your area contains a viewpoint like a hill or a climbable rock, spend some time at the top taking in the landscape as a whole.

Identifying Pulse Points

Pulse points of the landscape are places where earth energies collect and can be accessed; they are the points where we can communicate directly with the land and its spirits. Large sections of landscape will have several such nodes or pulse points, while a small backyard may have only a single weak one.

1. Within your chosen area, begin by identifying the places where you feel most inclined to sit and look around, and the places you look forward to seeing each time you go.

2. As you visit each of these places, spend a few moments sitting still, observing the energies around you. A pulse point should feel like a protected "heart" of the landscape that embodies or reflects its specialness. Wide-open vistas or viewpoints are helpful for scanning

---

*Ted Andrews, *Animal-Speak* (St. Paul, Minn.: Llewellyn Publications, 1993).

the landscape and learning about its interrelationships but are usually too exposed to serve as effective pulse points.

3. If several areas feel like pulse points, begin with the one that seems the strongest. Make another offering of cornmeal or seeds to the spirit of the land. As you do so, give thanks for being able to be present on this land and share in its beauties. Continue to make offerings to other pulse points in your chosen landscape.

PART III

Treatment

Druid Magic

I was out working in the yard when Ivan and his friend Lucie arrived in the late afternoon. They climbed from the car, marveling at the woodsy beauty of our surroundings. My yard *was* particularly lovely this afternoon, I noted. I greeted Lucie, who seemed shy, with a tentative hug and then turned to meet Ivan, who was so tall and bighearted that tentativeness was out of the question. A Celtic giant with a ready smile and a mop of white-gold curls, Ivan bent himself over to hug me, radiating warmth and a sense of mischief. This was fun already.

The air was alive with twittering birds, and flowers were blooming everywhere—pink and purple sweet peas, tiny white roses in the hedge, and enormous fuchsia peonies bobbing at our knees and perfuming the air. The woods across the road were dark and wet, and everywhere around us the landscape was wrapped in swaths of living greens—pine needles and maple leaves, tall oaks, blueberry bushes, climbing grapevines, overgrown hedges, blackberry thickets, and infinite other bushes, trees, and grasses whose names I didn't know.

A forty-foot cherry tree was in full bloom by the front door; it shimmered with the electric buzz of what sounded like a thousand bees working over its blossoms. I was glad that the landscape was putting on such a fine show for my guests; the beauty of the day put us all at ease, and we fell into comfortable chitchat before I'd even taken them inside.

As Ivan and Lucie had been driving for most of the day, they rested while I cooked dinner. Afterward we took a walk, and I told my guests about Indian Point and the work I'd done thus far—the pulses, planting the crystals, the Hudson as Conception Vessel, and Dunderberg Mountain as the spiritual center of the area. I explained how I saw my job: as supporting the healthy energy of Dunderberg while reducing the distorted energy of Indian Point.

"This is what the land feels like around here when it's healthy," I told them, extending my arm out to indicate the land all around us. "Its beauty and tranquillity are palpable, almost a physical force of nourishment." I smiled at this and was relieved to see Ivan and Lucie smiling, too. No one thought I really meant beauty was for eating, but they seemed to understand my attempt to describe the environment as something nearly tangible.

"But when we see the area around Indian Point and Dunderberg Mountain tomorrow," I continued, "you'll see how this beauty has twisted. The power is still there, but it has turned negative and scary." I paused, unsure how to communicate the scary reality of Indian Point to these people who lived so far away from it.

"Power is mutable," said Ivan gently, his British accent rolling the words out into the evening air. "It can be channeled toward healing, even if it seems frightening at first." And with that, something settled deeply in me; I felt comforted and realized that Ivan was the right person for this job. He understood the magnitude of what we were attempting, but he was not afraid. I glanced at Lucie, who was looking at Ivan. Perhaps she, too, was seeing his strength in that moment.

The next day we were up early. Ivan suggested that we assemble a small shrine in my living room and make some opening prayers before we embarked on our busy day. I was happy to follow his lead. Though I had worked hard to bring the project to this point, I was now ready for someone else's input. I was glad that Ivan was ready to take charge of the tone of the day, from the opening prayers onward.

I showed Ivan the table that I used as my meditation altar. He moved the candle and water and cornmeal around, then added his own

Druidic touches: a bowl of crystals from Tintagel—the birthplace of King Arthur—a small statue of a dragon, and a brown glass bottle of plant spirit medicine. He spoke some words of prayer, stating our gratitude for the many influences that had brought us to this day, and our intent to help heal the Hudson River and surrounding areas to benefit all the beings. We extinguished the candle, then were on our way.

Our first stop was the riverfront in Cold Spring. Just fifteen minutes from my house, the waterfront boasted a viewing pavilion that extended out into the river, so that there was water on three sides and peerless views to the north and south of the Hudson Highlands. I wanted Ivan and Lucie to see the river at its best—as they had seen the landscape at its best—so they would have a sense of the beauty that was the original condition of this area.

They quietly absorbed the scenery. Just as at my house I had the sense that both Ivan and Lucie were seeing deeply into the landscape, adjusting themselves to its nuances and quickly developing a feel for the river. As though I were bringing new friends to meet old ones, I breathed a sigh of relief that the introduction was going well. So much *didn't* need to be said, because they understood the magnificence of the place right away.

Lucie had suggested I bring along some milk to offer the river, so I said a quick prayer and poured a cool white stream into the turbid flow. Soon the milk disappeared. "And where is the power plant in relation to here?" asked Ivan. "Will the milk get there?"

"Yes," I told him. Indian Point was only twelve miles downstream, although we couldn't see it from where we stood because of the river's sharp turns. The tide was ebbing, so the downstream flow was relatively rapid.

"Then I know just what to do," Ivan exclaimed, pulling a small brown bottle from his jacket like a magician finding coins. I recognized the bottle that had been on our shrine a few minutes before. "I'll send some medicine into the river," explained Ivan, "and it will slowly make its way into the intake valves of the power plant, spreading messages of love and light.

"Allheal is my main medicine," he continued. "It has been popular with Druids for thousands of years, known for its general healing properties and its ability to neutralize poisons." He dripped three careful drops into the river and smiled. "Hard to imagine sometimes how these tiny drops can affect something so large as a power station—let alone a river. But magic isn't troubled by matters of scale. One wish is as good, or better, than a thousand."

I drove Ivan and Lucie to Jones Point. On the way I told them how the area seemed to concentrate the woes of the power plant, but I was inwardly worried that they wouldn't see what I meant. Nothing was visibly wrong with the place, except for Indian Point looming across the way. Would they understand?

I needn't have worried. As we began our descent toward Jones Point from Bear Mountain, Ivan and Lucie grew quiet. We got out of the car at the riverside, and Ivan remarked at the horrible feeling he was having. Lucie said she felt oppressed. Ivan pointed out some lines of black energy that he saw and snapped a few photos. I didn't really know what he was seeing in those lines of energy or what they meant, but I didn't feel that I needed to know either. I wanted to let him do his own diagnostics, in whatever way he preferred to do them.

Finally we went to Dunderberg Mountain. I offered tobacco and cornmeal at the gateway of trees at the beginning of the trail and said a short prayer. We climbed the first part of the trail, and I told Ivan and Lucie how this mountain seemed to be the genius loci of the region, but somehow lay dormant. I explained our notion of waking the mountain, so that it could equalize and counter the overpowering energy of Indian Point. Just at that moment, we rounded the small switchback trail that brought us directly in front of the power plant. I saw Lucie startle with surprise, as I had done the first time I saw that view. Ivan looked thoughtful. "I think you would need something as big as a mountain to match that power station," he said.

We continued on up the mountain, not stopping again until we reached the double helix where I had imagined a small stone circle could be built. We could just glimpse Indian Point through the overhanging leaves, but at this height and distance it did not seem threatening. Ivan noted that the trees created a natural window between this spot and the power station, and that it felt like a portal connecting the two spaces. I showed them the spot at this overlook where James and I had recently planted a large crystal, which had mysteriously disappeared by the time of our next visit. I was quite disturbed by this disappearance; it didn't seem possible that someone could be following me around and undoing my efforts at healing, but whoever had managed to come across my crystal had taken it away, and this made me feel vulnerable. There was a break in the security boundary, and I didn't know where it was or how to protect myself.

Ivan planted a small crystal there. "This crystal comes from Tintagel,"* he said, "the magical place in Cornwall where Merlin spun his magic so that King Arthur would be conceived. In this spot we hope to conceive another new beginning," he nodded across the river to the power plant, "a healing energy between these two places."

This was astonishing. Other than mentioning the Conception Vessel by name, I had not told Ivan about the many references to conception and birth that had arisen during the work thus far: the image of the "nut-brown mother" I had seen giving birth the first time James and I had visited this spot; the cell-division/double-helix shape of the clearing where we stood; the notion of the Hudson as the Conception Vessel of acupuncture; even the phallic shape of the power plant itself. Yet Ivan had felt called to bring powerful magic of conception to this place. What would come of it? I wondered. What, exactly, was on the cusp of being conceived?

Ivan placed three drops of allheal on top of the crystal he had planted, and Lucie added some flower essences of her own. I said a prayer of thanks to the ancestors of the many magical traditions that had led the three of us to this place, with these medicines, and added a

---

*Pronounced tin-'ta-jul.

note about new birth. "Whatever is trying to be born here, may it benefit all the beings of this region and bring them greater joy."

We continued up the trail. At one of the graded beds of the old spiral railway, I was struck anew by the enormous wall of rock that bordered the evenly graded ground. I couldn't tell if the rock had been blasted away for the railway, or whether it had just formed this way—as a giant gateway or palisade, its steep edge seemingly carved with faces of all kinds. Human and animal faces, giants and insects—eyes, noses, ears, and mouths seemed to reach out of the rock toward us. We stopped and stared. "It is the rock-beings of the mountain coming to greet us," said Lucie in her soft voice. "Let's greet them back." And she began to sing a simple chant—a heart-opening song of connection and compassion that is part of the Cherokee tradition.

As the song echoed in my ears, I realized that Ivan, Lucie, and I were already beginning to wake the mountain. I had kind of thought that I was taking them on a fact-finding journey this day—that I was showing them some sites, so that we could plan what would happen at a later date: where we would build the stone circle, where and when the healing would happen. But as those beings of the mountain stared down at us, I understood that this *was* the medicine. *We were already beginning.*

I was suddenly overcome with humility and gratitude for having so many wonderful helpers for this project. Venerable Dhyani and James, now Ivan and Lucie—wise and strong souls, both—who had been willing to travel far and put themselves on this mountain with me to meet whatever came. When the song was finished, we felt that these guardians of the mountain had given us their blessings and had bidden us to go further on the journey.

As we ascended the final rise of the trail, we heard a strange huffing sound in the woods ahead of us. It took me a minute to remember where I'd heard that sound before. "It's a deer," I explained. "That's about as aggressive as they get. I'm not sure what it's trying to tell us." We slowed down but kept walking, then heard something crashing through the brush ahead of us. We rounded a bend in the trail and stopped short, assailed by a ripe and fetid odor.

Every woman knows this smell; it is the smell of menstrual blood, of childbirth—a strong soup of life and death—fear mingled with joy, pain with transcendence. Sure enough, there was a tiny still-wet fawn curled in the middle of the trail. For a moment we stood in shock, not sure if we were seeing life or death—the delicate boundary between them having been so recently crossed. The little fawn quivered in the new air, the pounding *huff* of its surprised mother still sounding in our ears. Slowly the world righted itself, and we saw the great magic that we had been allowed to witness: new life, new life, *new life*.

We had been gifted with a rare privilege, the joy of it hard to assimilate: who gets to see a deer born in the wild? Conception energy indeed! We sang a song and went on our way, hoping the mother deer had not gone too far away and would be back to care for her little one.

We continued up the mountain and soon found ourselves at the top of the trail, overlooking the whole Hudson Highlands and Indian Point far below. Diffuse sunshine bathed the afternoon in a kind of glow. Butterflies darted about, and birdsong echoed through the air. "Perfect place for a picnic," Ivan suggested, so I began to unpack the sandwiches and fruit we'd brought along for lunch. We sat down in the soft grass and began to eat. On closer inspection, the grass we were sitting on was actually a carpet of dark moss, spotted here and there with teeny white flowers—like stars in a night sky.

"I'm surprised that we are seeing so many delicate little things here," said Lucie. "Tiny flowers and butterflies, newborn deer . . . they are so life affirming in this place. Even though down below the power plant feels so antagonistic to life, up here it is a different story." I explained to Ivan and Lucie that James and I had had a similar revelation up here, noting that the power plant seemed kind of harmless at this remove.

"It's amazing what a change of perspective can do," agreed Ivan. "What once looked overwhelming can become simply a situation that calls to be addressed." With his magician's flourish, Ivan reached into a pocket somewhere and pulled out a flute. "This beauty calls for a song of thanks," he said, and began to play a piping summer tune as he danced around on the grass. Joy seemed to bubble out from him in all directions. I'd never seen an adult express happiness so playfully, so spontaneously, and so . . . Celticly. This was ancient woodland magic in another idiom—not the Chinese medicine that had informed so much of the project thus far, nor the Native wisdom that had shaped this place for millennia.

I stared at the perfect river far below and ached for a perfect world to mirror it. As the last notes of Ivan's flute drifted away on the breeze, I felt compelled to sing an old song, though I didn't understand why at the time. I just opened my mouth and let the song come out:

> "B-y the w-a-ters, the waters of Babylon,
> We lay down and wept, and wept, for thee Zion.
> We remember, we remember, we remember thee Zion."

As I sang, I saw the Hudson River in its pristine state. I "remembered" the healthy, joyful, rolling river as it had been before its exile— before the people had plundered its riches and polluted its grace. I told the river that we remembered, we remembered its original perfect beauty, and we wept for its losses.

I marveled that this song was also a hymn of my Jewish heritage— another strand of cultural DNA woven into this polyglot project. When I finished, the air was still. Then a bald eagle lifted up from a tree below us and flew across our entire field of vision from left to right. "We have noticed you," the eagle's flight seemed to be telling us. "We hereby acknowledge your work here."

Ivan, Lucie, and I walked down the mountain quietly, each absorbed in our own thoughts. At the clearing where I had imagined the stone circle would be built, we stopped for a few minutes. I found myself in a very open and gentle state, staring across the river at the power plant with something like love in my heart. *We are in this together,* I thought to myself. *Growing together.* Then without warning came a stab of fear so acute that it felt like pain. If I really let myself love that thing, what would happen to me? Would I get poisoned by the radiation? Would I develop cancer? I didn't want to let it in, not like that. So I pushed it away. *I am not ready to love it. I don't want to let it penetrate,* I thought to myself. But still I felt scared. Something of it had jumped across into me at that moment, and I felt marked.

On the way home from Dunderberg, I stopped at the Capuchin monastery grounds to show Ivan and Lucie the circle of elder trees. This was the only place, other than Dunderberg, that had seemed a possibility for a stone circle, and I wanted Ivan to see it. The dappled wood with its circle of giants was a paragon of stability and unflappability. Ivan marveled at the grandfather tree, which he judged to be about three hundred years old. Then he played the flute for a few moments, and the sweet song dipped around in the air like an aural butterfly.

"Does this place correspond to a specific acupuncture point, like the area on Dunderberg?" Lucie asked. I hadn't considered that before; it was an interesting question. I thought fast. Those strong trees, presiding over the landscape, working to shield it from the encroachments of the mechanized world. That was kind of a heart protector function. The enclosed, contemplative nature of this place also fit in with a heart protector role, which guards the spirit.

"This is a Heart Protector point," I answered, still working out the details in my mind. "Maybe Heart Protector 6 or 7." Interestingly, this heart protector landscape felt almost the complete opposite of the blown-open defenselessness of the Heart pulse at the Kitchawan reservoir. I was glad to see some strength here. "Perhaps some of the serenity of this heart protector can be channeled toward the heart of the Hudson," I suggested, "to remind it that it is safe and surrounded by a circle of protection."

"Shall we put in some crystal needles, then?" Ivan offered. I nodded in assent. Ivan chose a large triangle of moss just outside the tree circle as a good location for his work and knelt down beside it. Lucie and I stood near the triangle's other two sides. Ivan carefully planted a crystal on each side of the triangle, then looked up at Lucie and me. "It doesn't feel complete, somehow," he ventured. "Perhaps we should plant another crystal in the center of the triangle."

As best we could, we measured out where the center point fell, and Ivan pulled a beautiful Tintagel crystal from his bag. The moment he placed it in the ground, church bells pealed around us in a counter-phonic song. We stared at each other in surprise—the soundtrack could not have been more precisely timed if we'd planned it.

"What a perfect end to our day," said Ivan, the wonder audible in his voice. "I trust that our work has been accepted and welcomed by the spirits of the land all around us." We said a prayer of humble thanks, to acknowledge the power greater than ourselves who was keeping such a close eye on our work and giving us such sure feedback. And then we headed home.

That night, I had a dream in which I was standing on Dunderberg Mountain looking over the river at the power plant. The plant sparkled like a crystal in the sunshine, and waves of relief and joy flowed out of it into the air and water all around. I woke up filled with happiness and humility at the thought that our unscripted adventure had had such an immediate and lovely effect on the power plant, and the river beside it. Ivan reported that he'd had a significant dream that night as well: he was working in a laboratory, wearing a white lab coat. On a table in the lab was a model of the power station; he was redesigning it to make it safer and more friendly to the environment.

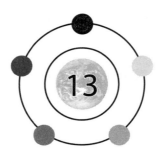

The In Breath

The next morning, Ivan gave me a brief summary of his thoughts about our work the previous day and what he imagined would be needed next. He noted first of all the astonishing number and surprising nature of the signs we'd encountered the day before—most notably the birth of the deer, the eagle flying overhead, and the church bells at the oak circle. "These are signals of great power," he pointed out, "and they indicate to me that the land is very responsive to our work, and indeed very eager for it." This eagerness on the part of the land made Ivan feel good about participating in this project and excited about the next stage.

"I'd like to come back in a few months' time and build a small stone circle at that clearing on Dunderberg Mountain," Ivan continued. "And I'd like to bring my friend Patrick along as well." He explained that Patrick is a geomancer who has a lot of experience with earth energies and would have a great deal to contribute to a project of this scale and intensity.

"Is this Patrick MacManaway?" I asked, wondering if this was the same healer that Venerable Dhyani had suggested I contact all those months ago. Ivan nodded. "Yes, I took the liberty of speaking to Patrick about you when I first got your letter. He's very interested to work on a project of this magnitude, and we would do well to include him."

"Yes, that's perfect," I sputtered in surprise, amazed that fortune had conspired to bring me the very person I wanted to find. "When can you come?" We settled on a three-day window in early August—exactly two months away. I helped Ivan and Lucie pack up and hugged them as they went on their way. It had been an astonishing and exhausting couple of days, and I was glad I'd have some time to integrate my experience.

A few days later, I decided to go back to the oak grove to sit in the peace and beauty that Ivan, Lucie, and I had discovered there. I would think about the project and try to figure out what, if anything, needed to be done before Ivan and Patrick came in August. Standing by the mossy triangle where we had given thanks and planted crystals, I recalled that astonishing second when the church bells rang—exactly at the moment that Ivan planted the center crystal. I tried to let my body resound with the memory of that bell and with the council of trees nearby. Then I sat on a rock in the sunshine, tuned in with Dunderberg and the river, and posed a question: What *should* I be doing right now, in these weeks before building the stone circle?

I began with a review of what I had done thus far. I had taken pulses and listened to the landscape; this was like the intake I do with each client at the beginning of a session. Next, I had identified Moheakantuk as a specific meridian—the Conception Vessel—and found its opening point on Dunderberg Mountain. This was analogous to choosing a treatment strategy and points to needle.

The third stage—the work I had just completed with Ivan and Lucie—was kind of like palpating the meridians and points on a client to find the exact place to needle. In my treatment room, I will select a point to needle, then palpate around it with my fingers—sometimes so lightly that my fingers hardly touch the skin, other times quite deeply. With this quiet activity I am accomplishing multiple things; most importantly, perhaps, I am beginning to engage more deeply with the client's energy body. My intentions are now beginning to shape the treatment, which has already begun.

At this stage I am also searching for the exact place where the needle will be most effective; a textbook point location can be a field as large as several inches, while the actual point of a needle is quite tiny.

Good point location can make the difference between a powerful treatment and an ineffective one. During this focused palpation, I am also listening quite intently for further helpful information—subtle changes in skin texture or temperature around the point, comments from the client that may yield important clues about his ailments, and my own inner guidance about what needs to be done and how.

All of these details seemed characteristic of my day with Ivan and Lucie, and the careful attention we had paid to the mountain as we cautiously explored it and began to offer medicine in the form of song, flower essences, and prayers. What needed to happen next?

In an acupuncture session, the next thing I do is plant my feet squarely on the floor and take a deep breath, in and out, to clear my thoughts and attachments. What matters now is becoming one with the nature of healing. Then I inhale and connect with the earth and the sky. In the moment of this in breath I draw energy up from Mother Earth through my legs, and down from Father Sky through the crown of my head and neck. The primordial yin and yang energies meet and mix in my heart.

For a moment I hold this energy, hold my breath, and focus on the human being in front of me, on his or her journey of growth and healing. In this moment of stillness, if all goes well, I cease to be me; I merge with the future, with the healing that is to come. Then I focus my eyes and energy on the acupuncture point—a tiny spot that opens like a gateway—and I exhale, releasing the gathered energies from my heart into my hands and thence to the needle, which moves swiftly like an arrow into the point.

This dance of breath and energy is repeated with each needle: every treatment is a meditation, an affirmation of my role as a transducer of yin and yang, of earth and sky, into the universal current that is known—like God—by many names in many places: *qi, prana, life force, light, love.*

This time of waiting for Ivan and Patrick was like that moment of the in breath. A time to clear myself and attune to the energies that would be the true healers of this land. It was a beautiful image, and one that left me feeling that the landscape was ready for the next stage of work—the acupuncture treatment that would happen when we built the stone circle at Dunderberg.

I spent the next several weeks in a quiet rhythm of work and gardening, enjoying the uneventful time as I looked forward to the upcoming adventure with Ivan and Patrick. Then something shifted—on a camping trip with friends in early July, I found myself anxious, sleepless, and irritable. I came home exhausted and angry with myself for being unable to relax, and sunburned; the upper part of my chest was annoyingly red and warm as I fell into bed that night.

The next morning, after another restless night, I woke with a throbbing headache and a neck so stiff that I could barely turn my head. In the mirror I noticed the isolated patch of sunburn on my chest, still hot to the touch, but strange, too, because my face wasn't burned at all. How had I managed to sunburn just my chest? I pulled my shirt aside to investigate the burn and found a looping line of red that stretched to my right arm. I followed it, turning around to see a large red ring draped over my shoulder and the side of my neck. With a sinking feeling I realized that this was not sunburn, but a rash. On closer inspection, it was a classic bull's-eye rash—a marker of Lyme disease. I hadn't known these rashes could be so big, but it was undeniable. Uh-oh.

Having already seen too many clients with persistent, debilitating Lyme, I knew that it was not to be trifled with. I could take herbs to help rebuild my strength later, but right now I needed antibiotics; it seemed that the longer this disease went untreated, the worse it got. I managed to schedule an appointment with a doctor that afternoon and said only, "I think I have Lyme disease," before showing him the rash. He raised his eyebrows in surprise and told me he was going to presume Lyme, though only the blood work would tell for sure. I gratefully filled and started the antibiotic prescription he gave me and spent the next few days in a haze.

I had not taken antibiotics in at least fifteen years and was at once heartened and incapacitated by their power. Whatever they were doing to me was wracking my body. I was nauseous and shaky and unable to think a sensible thought or sleep for more than an hour at a time. My head hurt and I was painfully sensitive to light. I canceled my clients for a few days and just lay on the couch, letting the time pass. I was not surprised to get a call from the nurse telling me that my Lyme test was clearly positive, showing quite high antibody levels. "You're a pretty sick puppy," she said, meaning to be kind. As if I didn't already know.

For days I did little but stumble between the couch and the bed, taking inventory of my many symptoms. When I was able to have a coherent thought, I found I was worrying about the spiritual significance of my illness; was it somehow a sign that I should stop working on the stone circle? Had I taken on more than I could handle? Alternatively, was some dark force trying to prevent me from completing this healing work? I considered all of these possibilities, but none seemed to resonate. Although it was tempting to be able to blame my sickness on something outside of me—a dark force or an insistent sign—I sensed that the truth was a lot more complex.

I kept thinking about that day in the oak grove—those ticks crawling over my body—and my confused feelings of love and fear. The confusion had made me vulnerable, I felt sure, but beyond that I couldn't figure out why I had fallen so ill so fast. One day, I realized that my moment of uncertainty in looking at those ticks was familiar—it was similar to the feeling I'd had looking at Indian Point that day with Ivan and Lucie, when I'd been so frightened of what the power plant might do to me if I truly allowed myself to love it. In both of these instances, I'd been grappling with a question of how to love something that can hurt me: this was a heart protector issue, plain and simple.

Now it occurred to me that the shock and repulsion I'd felt at the thought of the power plant invading me is perhaps what I *should have* felt looking at those ticks. Maybe I should have pushed them away with physical and emotional force, as I had the power plant. Or at least reaffirmed my body as a sacred space that would not tolerate invaders. Instead, I had been reluctant to protect myself, unable to establish my strength as inviolate, and had left myself vulnerable. This was indeed a heart protector issue, and I had fallen prey to it sitting at a Heart Protector point. How could I have been so careless?

In any kind of healing or shamanic work it is important for practitioners to protect themselves from the energies of others. I had heard this countless times and had witnessed the protection rituals of many different practitioners. But I had never gone in much for protection rituals myself; it felt unseemly, or melodramatic somehow. Unenlightened, even, with its focus on what we should be afraid of instead of how we might transform negative energies into light.

Instead, I had believed that if I just kept my heart in the right place, everything would be okay. Now I saw that belief as a form of denial. I hadn't spent any time thinking about what "not okay" might look like, nor had I imagined the many kinds of vectors by which unhealthy influences might reach me. I just didn't think about it. Now I was paying the price.

It would take years of partial recovery before I finally realized that Lyme disease, like radiation, is nearly impossible to get rid of. The spiral-shaped bacteria that cause Lyme are able to bury themselves deeply in their host's tissues, coat themselves in the host's immune proteins, and even change their form to a type that is invulnerable to antibiotics. Lyme can cause permanent damage to nerve and muscle tissue and, for many people, becomes a chronic illness with periods of quiescence and flare-up. Learning to live with Lyme is like learning to live with a nuclear power plant in your backyard: when all the containment strategies are in place, you can function almost normally, but one system failure can easily trigger a cascade of others, and the possibility of a "meltdown" is ever present.

At the time, I didn't know any of this and had a simple faith in the power of antibiotics to make me well. And this was partially true at first. After five or six days of medicine I did begin to feel better, and by the time my three-week prescription was done I felt fatigued and somewhat anxious, but otherwise functional and ready for Ivan and Patrick's visit in a few days' time.

Around this time I received a call from Lucie, who explained that she would not be able to join us for the building of the stone circle. I was greatly disappointed; Lucie had been a great companion on that earlier work with Ivan, and I'd been counting on her returning when Ivan came back with Patrick. Her absence would leave yin and yang quite imbalanced, as I would now be the only woman working with Ivan, Patrick, and James. This arrangement seemed unstable to me.

I wondered what other female I could bring in at the last minute. I thought of Laura and how much better I would feel if she were able to join us. But I knew the energy of Indian Point would be poison for a woman trying to get pregnant; I wouldn't ask her to do something that felt so wrong. Still, perhaps there was another way that I could bring Laura in and also correct the yin-yang ratio a little bit; maybe Laura could help me make the bundles that Venerable Dhyani had recommended I place beneath each stone of the circle. The gathering of cedar, quartz crystals, and a pinch of cornmeal wrapped in a red cloth was by nature a very yin exercise; the making of the bundles would be a good time to establish a yin and feminine foundation for the stones.

I invited Laura to make bundles with me, and she was happy to help. On the day before Ivan and Patrick were to arrive, Laura walked in my door with a giant smile and a thatch of cedar boughs, and we set up a workshop for ourselves on the floor of my living room. Laura was the perfect companion for this project. A gifted visual artist and a deeply feminine being, in no time at all she had shifted and worked the elements of the bundle until she found a way to make them beautiful together.

We called in our ancestors and the wise protective guardians of the four directions. We called to the river and the mountain, and to all the creatures that swim and fly and crawl and walk on the land and waters of the Hudson rivershed. I thanked Venerable Dhyani and all of the elders who had helped me bring this healing to manifest. I thanked all of the people who had contributed their love and support. I thanked Ivan and Lucie and James and Laura and Patrick, all of those who walked with me on this journey. I thanked the Indian Point nuclear power plant and its legions of well-intentioned workers. I prayed that the bundles we were about to assemble would hold all of these healing energies and broadcast them out through the shining stones we would place above them. And then Laura and I began to build. Cornmeal bundle, cedar twig, crystal, wrapped in a red thread. Twelve bundles for twelve stones, and a thirteenth for the center stone.

When we were done I felt as though we'd woven some primordial life force into those bundles; though tiny, they seemed to vibrate with intention and power. I lay them carefully in a carved wooden box and placed it on my meditation shrine. Laura and I hugged goodbye; we knew we had done a good job, and nothing more needed to be said. I went to bed that night satisfied that I was prepared for the coming days.

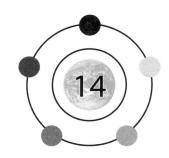

Acupuncture for the Earth

When Ivan and Patrick arrived at my house on a humid August evening, they were lit up with excitement about the terrific thunderstorms they'd driven through on their journey. Ivan gestured wildly with his hands to describe the bolts of lightning and incredible rain; Patrick smiled in quiet wonder. The two friends were a perfect yin-and-yang pair: Ivan tall and fair and larger than life; Patrick quiet and watchful, his power rolling out from him in deliberate movements and a soft, gentle voice. He remarked that they'd been given a magnificent demonstration of the Earth's power, and a keen reminder of the deep work we would be doing the following day. I felt proud to be in their company.

In the two minutes it took us to drive from Jones Point to the trailhead at Dunderberg, the sky grew darker. Heavy black clouds were accumulating to the north and west of us, just behind the mountain. Patrick, Ivan, James, and I climbed from the car into a wall of hot, damp air. Everything around me felt compressed; normal sounds and movements seemed muffled and tight; even the light looked somehow squeezed. I took a deep breath and felt, inside, surprisingly free of the atmospheric tension building so vividly around me. Instead I felt energized and singularly focused—almost in motion already, as though in the unstoppable middle of a footstep or a flight. This day was the culmination of events put into play a long time ago; now the forces arrayed within and around us were pushing for the work to be completed.

Reviewing our packs and supplies, Ivan nodded approvingly, telling us that we looked convincingly like a bunch of hippies out for a hike. "The guards at the plant who watch those hidden cameras all day shouldn't take much notice of us," he ventured. "Especially in the dark and stormy gloom."

I hadn't realized that Ivan worried, too, about being watched by guards or police—but I was glad he'd been thinking about it. Although we weren't doing anything wrong or illegal, building a stone circle across the river from Indian Point suddenly felt like a very subversive act. We knew that the forces of magic and medicine we were invoking have historically been very threatening to the powers that be, including governments, military organizations, and the church. Through the ages, such organizations have responded to humble earth magic with repression and outright violence, neither of which we wanted to invite. Yet in the heightened reality of the day, anything seemed possible. Better to stay under the radar altogether.

Thoughts of being challenged before we could finish our work added a note of excitement to our already-prickling senses. We walked toward the trailhead with bright faces and purposeful minds. At the entrance to the trail we paused in front of the young trees that arched above our heads to form a visible gate. I sprinkled a bit of tobacco on the ground and Ivan poured a few drops of allheal near the trees' roots. I greeted the mountain and asked permission to complete the healing work we had promised. Dunderberg's answer came quickly in a roll of thunder that barreled across the sky above our heads.

We looked at each other nervously. This was the first thunder we'd heard all day. "Do we take that as an invitation or a threat?" I wondered aloud.

"Well, the mountain definitely knows we're here," said Ivan thoughtfully, "but I don't get the sense that we're being asked to leave. If that were the case I'd expect something even more formidable, like a fire, or a car accident, or a lightning strike. Nature spirits have some pretty direct ways of letting us know when we're not wanted."

"That's true," James pointed out, as he turned to me. "Do you remember those times we tried to climb the mountain and couldn't?" Images from our first attempts to climb the mountain flashed through my mind—once we couldn't find the trail, and several times the weather was so bad we never even left our houses. This was not really like that, just a little warning.

"I see what you mean," I agreed. This thunder didn't feel like an obstacle, more like a stern glare. "I think we've gotten permission to come in," I said, "but also a reminder that we've stirred up some serious energies, and we're not to take it lightly."

"Well done," said Patrick softly. "I think you've hit it exactly. Let's remember that the mountain and all the beings around us have an interest and a stake in what we're doing." We moved along the trail in silence. The woods were damp, and it was something of a struggle to step through the wet underbrush and heavy air. Each of us was absorbed in our own thoughts. As we began to climb the hill, I found myself conscious of each breath and the sound of my footsteps on the ground. More thunder rolled, and we grinned crazily at one another, excited now at the magnitude of the energies that were unleashing themselves around us.

We rounded one of the small trail's switchbacks and stopped, shocked, to see a woman and her two young children picking late raspberries. It seemed such an innocent activity in this dark and brooding place. We exchanged startled smiles and hellos before moving past each other. I wondered how strange we must have looked to her, intently filing up the mountain in a growing storm.

Soon it began to rain. And rain harder. Patrick wondered if we wanted to continue on or look for shelter for a little while. We paused to consider. "The old train tunnel is just ahead," I said, pointing it out. "We could wait in there for a while." Everyone peered through the downpour, trying to discern the cavelike mouth of the tunnel. "Let's see how it feels," said James, and led the way.

The tunnel was dry and dark. Silent at first, we put down our packs and took seats on the rocks and logs that seemed to have been placed there for that purpose. We listened to the deluge for many minutes. After a while Patrick and Ivan began to look around, wondering about the provenance of our strange shelter. I told them what I had read—about the tunnel being a remnant of the minirailroad a company had begun to install in the 1890s, hoping to turn Dunderberg Mountain into a tourist resort, similar to the Bear Mountain Lodge up the road. "But they never completed it," I added, "and the project was eventually abandoned."

"I'm not the least bit surprised," said Ivan wryly. "The spirit of Dunderberg doesn't seem like it would tolerate a frivolous venture like that. A chemistry lab, maybe, but a tourist park . . . I don't see it." In the general chuckle that followed I began to feel a slight buzz in my head. Something didn't feel right. Our laughter and random conversation began to grate on my nerves. "I think our rest stop might be done," I said. "Perhaps we need a short prayer to reconnect us to what we're doing." Everyone agreed, and we sang a chant that would open our hearts and connect each of us to the hearts of all beings. The simple tones echoed around us in the tunnel for several moments after we stopped singing. I heard Patrick remark that the rain didn't seem to be letting up.

"It may be time to get moving anyway," he said to Ivan. "What do you think?" As Ivan began to answer, I felt that buzzing in my head again and an insistent tug at my awareness. The cold and empty fire pit loomed in front of me, pleading. "It wants a fire," I said, suddenly understanding the message I'd been getting from . . . somewhere. "Ivan, will you do the honors?"

Ivan had a special relationship with fire, and in fact seemed part fire himself. Twice struck by lightning, he generally radiated a kinetic, electrical energy and warmth. That and his Druid's fascination with dragons, who are creatures of fire, made him seem the natural choice for one to kindle a fire in this damp and dark tunnel. Under his mild direction, we gamely assembled the driest twigs and branches we could find. Ivan compiled the kindling with great care and lit several matches, but the fire gave only smoke for a long time.

"Let's everyone focus on this fire," he suggested at last, "and see if we can't get it burning a bit more strongly." The four of us clustered around the smoky fire pit, calling inwardly to the images of warmth and light that came to each of us. Slowly the flames caught and began to generate warmth and light.

"That's better," said Ivan, before lapsing into silence like the rest of us, watching the fire-beings turn and dance in the flames. Strangely, the rain outside began to slow exactly as the fire increased. Within minutes we had a perfect, small fire and no more rain. After another short minute or two the sun came out.

"Well," said Patrick in his soft Scottish brogue, "I guess we have passed that particular test. The rain has stopped, and we are ready to move on to the next phase of our day's work." We put out the fire, picked up our packs, and stepped out of the cave into a wood that shimmered with water and light. As we stood there squinting at the sudden brightness, an enormous noise shook the air—a creaking and a rushing followed by a loud boom! We looked at each other in surprise that bordered on alarm as we tried to process the noise, when it came again—exactly the same way. Creak, crash, boom! Earthquake? Bombs?

"Trees falling," said Ivan, the first to decode the sound. "Two of them. You can still see branches shaking over there," he pointed across a gully. I could see leaves quivering amid a small patch of motion that was different from the stillness of the forest. I could also see Ivan and Patrick looking at each other, trying to interpret the meaning of these trees falling. Those two big crashes were echoing around my head, reminding me of something. I realized with a start what they sounded like—movie sound effects: the one where the door of the jail cell closes with a bang and the character knows he's locked in for good. Or the door of a haunted house, slamming shut as soon as the daring teenagers have stepped inside. *Ka-lang.*

"Well, we're *in*," I said, not sure whether to be glad or scared. "We're in for the duration."

We walked up the rest of the trail in silence, each of us considering the powerful ways that the mountain was acknowledging—and tracking— our presence. It was exciting to have such intense and immediate feedback to our every step, but it was also humbling. If the mountain could communicate this clearly with us now, how is it that we could have been so deaf to this conversation before now?

Was there a new faculty awakening in us on this day? A new awareness on the part of the mountain? Maybe both. Maybe the mountain really was waking up from some state of numbness or slumber, just as we were emerging from our state of human-centered ignorance. Together we were prodding one another into awareness.

At the landing where we would build the circle, we paused and surveyed the clearing. Ivan and Patrick conferred softly. "I'm going to do some earth acupuncture first," Patrick explained, "to balance the spot and help tune it in to the plant across the river."

He sat down on a low rock on the west side of the clearing and began to take things out of his pack. Without discussing why or where, the rest of us walked to the other cardinal directions and sat down: James to the north, Ivan in the east, and me in the south. I felt as though we were serving some role by sitting in the four directions— completing a circuit or guarding the space, or perhaps just bearing witness to Patrick's work. Though I wanted to know exactly what he was planning to do with the wooden and copper rods he began to unwrap, I felt it would be best not to disturb him with questions. Instead I would watch silently, supporting him with my focus and intention.

As I watched Patrick's fingers moving lightly over the ground, I imagined myself doing the same. I thought about how it is that I find the points on my clients. What is it that I do in those moments before the needle goes in?

Sometimes the points call. Not audibly, but visually or kinesthetically.

My fingers go first, but it is my eyes that home in to find the exact place. One spot looks darker, or weaker, or puffier. Cells of the skin seem to part to reveal a kind of a sinkhole where the needle should go. With the needle in my right hand, pointing like a laser toward the tiny invisible cavern, my left thumb and forefinger rest lightly on the skin, encircling the point. Inhale the energies of Mother Earth and Father Sky into my heart. Exhale, letting the energy flow down my arms into my hands, into the needle as it softly moves into the skin.

When I put the needles in I cannot *will* a change to happen. When it does happen, change unfolds according to some logic that is far larger than my conception of the issue, far outside the simple "if A, then B" mechanics of my human understanding. In this context, rooting for any specific outcome feels like an egoistic attempt to control the future, so I try not to do it. What I must do instead is recede, step back into the domain of an observer, committed to being in the moment with things as they are now. What do I see? What points are calling? How can I be of service?

I watched Patrick concentrating, manipulating the needles and looking around him with an unfocused stare. He, too, was an observer, witnessing the energies in his needles but not trying to control them. I felt a vague surprise that earth acupuncture could be so similar to the human variety, then surprise at myself—that I would still find this similarity surprising after so many months of finding exactly that.

"Well, that should do it," said Patrick, putting his needles away and rising. "The land feels attuned to us, and to the power plant, and ready for some stones. Let's let the work begin!" The four of us drew together in the clearing. "First we need to find the center of the circle," Patrick explained. "This is the heart of the circle and the heart of the medicine we are bringing to this landscape." He plucked one of the orange-tipped engineer's flags from a pile that Ivan had set on the ground and scanned his hands over the earth. In a moment he paused and pointed the flag to the ground as he pushed it in. It went in an inch or two before stopping. Patrick pushed at the flag but it went no farther.

"We'll need at least six or eight inches to bury the stone," said Ivan. "Finding the center is the first step in manifesting a new sacred space on Earth. It can take a bit of time. Let's keep trying." Patrick tried another point or two, but each time hit rock just a few inches below the surface. He then gave the flag over to Ivan, who broadened the search range a bit. "In my experience, there is only one possibility for the center of a stone circle," he said, "and we can embark on a process of elimination until we find it." After Ivan had hit rock two or three times as well, my hands began to tingle. I really wanted to try finding that center point but didn't want to insert myself into Patrick and Ivan's process. They had done this work together before, and I trusted that they would know how to move forward. Patrick tried one more time, then said, "Let's use the energies that we have. Why don't the three of us men hold hands in a circle around Gail and see if that works a bit better."

I stepped forward and took the flag from Patrick's hands, excited to be part of the action. Would I be able to find the center? Why hadn't Ivan and Patrick found it? As the men joined their hands in a circle around me I marveled at this completely new experience: having power handed to me by a group of men who deeply trusted me to take charge. This was the world as I knew it turned inside out, yet it felt just right.

I breathed deeply, then squatted down close to the wet earth and took the flag in my right hand like a needle. My left hand and eyes scanned the dirt, searching for the sinkhole—there. My eyes saw it first, fingertips confirming what I had already seen—the point where the skin of the earth was open, exactly like on a person. I breathed in, aligning the tip of the flag with the point, watching it yawn open to receive. Mother Earth, Father Sky, meeting in my heart. I exhaled, and in went the flag, down and down to a depth of eight or nine inches before it stopped. I paused in stillness, pleased with myself and proud. Yes, this is as it should be. I had been at the center of this project from the beginning and was integral to the center now. If the men were surprised, they didn't show it.

The ring of hands fell away around me, and I stepped back. The four of us stood and stared at the flag, getting acquainted with the center of our circle. I felt like a ship that had just dropped anchor—literally grounded to some substrate deep below. Patrick and Ivan exchanged glances, then nodded. "That feels goo-ood," Patrick said. "Very good."

"Right," exclaimed Ivan, bouncing over to his pack. "Now for the measuring and marking." He pulled out a tape measure and a ball of string. "I have found that twelve stones placed equidistantly around the center creates the most stabilizing force. Other shapes and configurations encourage different qualities of energy, but as we are trying to stabilize and harmonize the energies of this river valley, I believe the twelve-pointed star will be best.

"If it's all right with you," Ivan continued, nodding toward me, "Patrick and I will measure and mark the twelve positions now. We have done this work together before, and that seems the easiest way." I nodded. "It will take us some time," Ivan added. "Precision is very important in this kind of work. The earth and sky energies that we hope to call in are often best expressed in the exacting languages of number and geometry. We will take our time and get it correct, then join you for lunch." I hadn't thought about it before, but precise measurement *did* seem the only way to really engage energies of the magnitude we were aiming for. I was glad to have Ivan and Patrick's mastery available, and glad I didn't have to do the measuring. It would require a degree of focus that I couldn't imagine summoning up in this moment.

James and I walked over to our bags and unpacked the lunches we had brought, then perched on a low rock to eat. We barely spoke, just watched the two geomancers working their way through a complicated dance of angles and inches and degrees of arc, planting flags to mark the points. Once or twice they found themselves misaligned at opposite ends of the circle and had to backtrack until the locations were exact. When they were finished, they put away their tools, and I handed them their sandwiches.

Ivan sat down and shared with us some details of their siting work: rather than orienting the circle toward the cardinal points of the compass as they usually do, he and Patrick had decided to orient this circle toward the landscape. East was Indian Point, west was Dunderberg, and north and south were directions of the river. "So it's skewed a few degrees from the compass points," he finished, "but feels very well balanced overall." Patrick stood a few yards away, looking thoughtfully into the trees as he ate his lunch. I wondered what he was thinking about. What goes through the mind of a wizard in the moments between the magic?

The sky, which had remained dense but dry since we'd left the railway tunnel, now began to darken again. Ivan spent a few minutes gathering the thirteen stones that would make up our circle. He knew what he was looking for and found them nestled under trees or resting in piles, and carried them to a central spot outside the southwest corner of the circle. He handed out shovels and gardening trowels, and explained that he would pick the stone for each hole before we began to excavate it.

After offering a short prayer that our work be of benefit to the mountain and all the beings on and around it, we started in the west, with the Dunderberg stone. Ivan broke ground with a shovel, then the four of us set to work. Trowels went scraping in and bounced against rocks and roots. The digging was difficult, and we fought to bring up our shovelfuls of packed ground. There were so many large and small stones that we spent a lot of time excavating in order to be able to pull those rocks away. It began to rain again, and the music of the rain and the smell of the raw dirt were intoxicating as we pulled out shovelful after shovelful of wet earth. When Ivan judged that the hole was big enough, we stopped digging. I settled one of the bundles that Laura and I had made into the hole, and Ivan put in a Herkimer diamond and a few drops of allheal. He picked up the stone, and we all began to sing in simple tones. When he felt the time was right, Ivan set the stone into the hole; it hit with a deep and satisfying thud.

Ivan then led us across the circle to the eastern point, where we repeated the process. We continued this way for stone after stone in a deepening storm, and somewhere along the way seemed to slip into a mythical realm. In the dark wind and lashing rain we became like a pantheon of gods acting out the first steps of creation: thunder shook the air around us and lighting sliced across the sky as we scrabbled through the packed dirt laying stones, building mountains, planting seeds of the future. With each stone that I pulled from the fastened grip of the earth I felt myself trying to move infirmity—to claw the poisons of Indian Point from the places where it hides, to cleave molecule from molecule in an effort to rediscover a state of pure potential. Every stone that Ivan dropped into the ground became a visual poem—an arm reaching for the stars and touching a brighter future.

This, I realized, was as close to a definition of healing as I am ever likely to come—the moment of returning to pure potential, then arising again, transformed. Together, the four of us midwived this transformation thirteen times. After the thirteenth stone—the center stone, beneath which Ivan planted a Tintagel crystal alongside our bundle of magic—we stepped back in silence. We stared at our circle of stones, wondering if the effort and magic that had gone into building it would somehow be visible to the naked eye. Not really. This was a stealth circle, Ivan explained. Designed to do its work underground, out of sight of those who might find such a thing objectionable. While eight to twelve inches of rock lay buried at each position, only three or four inches of stone was visible in any one place. At that height, the rock blended in with the surrounding sticks and stones, looking randomly strewn about instead of laboriously planted. Good.

"We have one final step to complete in order to activate our circle," said Ivan. He had us stand around the center stone facing outward. "I will represent the spirit of Indian Point," he said, placing himself at the eastern edge, "and Patrick—you be the spirit of Dunderberg, facing west. James, you can stand facing south to represent the Hudson River downstream from here, and Gail, you face north, representing the Hudson River upstream." We all got into place and at Ivan's lead sang a plaintive song together, a simple vowel chant that seemed to weave the four directions into a harmonious blanket of sound.

"This is the first new moment," said Patrick as our music faded into the air. "And it is well blessed."

In a state of exultation and exhaustion we stumbled down the mountain in the rain and drove back to my quiet little house in the woods. It was warm and dry and . . . solid, not shimmering or numinous or shifting between worlds. I had never been more grateful for its unremarkable strength. We inhaled the wonderful dinner that my friend Jessica had cooked and delivered to us and spent a quiet evening sitting and talking, drinking hot tea, sorting through the day's experiences. Patrick suggested that we could check in with the mountain in about six months' time, to see how it was responding to our work. Six months sounded long, but geologic time, he reminded me, is different from human time. "The land could keep changing for years," he said. "A treatment like this will go deep, and the healing manifests over time."

In the morning, I felt as though I'd run a marathon—proud and pleased and achy as hell. As a farewell gift, Patrick dowsed his way around the yard and cleared my home of old and unfavorable energies. He worked as serenely as he had the day before: quietly, focused, and with a gentle goodwill that seemed to extend to everyone—even the old ghost he found pruning roses in the garden. "He is acting as a protector of this house," Patrick explained to me. "I can ask him to leave if you like, but he will not cause any harm and may in fact confer some benefit." I smiled wanly and nodded with surprise; *a friendly ghost, okay. I guess I have room for that.* The hazy summer air filled my brain and body; I felt enshrouded in fog and wanted to lie down.

As Ivan and Patrick got ready to leave I clasped their hands and searched for the words to express my gratitude. "Thank you for helping me to fulfill my pledge to the river," I began, then found myself choking up with emotion. "I really needed to do this, and I absolutely could not have done it without you. Thank you. Thank you so much." I smiled through tears and saw these two great men smiling kindly back at me, unhurried, and unembarrassed by my crying. I could not believe how lucky I was to have found them.

Ivan stepped forward and wrapped me in a big bear hug. "It has been wonderful to meet you and work with you," he said warmly. "I'm sure we will have more magical adventures together in the future." Then he swung his bags into the car as Patrick put his hands on my shoulders and kissed my cheeks three times, in the European way. He spoke each time our faces met: "Happy meet. Happy part. And happy meet again." I smiled and waved them on their way with a grin I could scarcely contain. Patrick's little spell had conjured up happiness!

I walked back into my house, wondering what the next six months would bring. I had no idea that my life would change completely in that time: I'd be sicker than I'd ever been and stretched to my limit in clawing my way back to health; I would meet the man I was going to marry; I would decide to leave the Hudson Valley. And the valley itself . . . would be engulfed in darkness, and would change the whole country's conversation about power and the energy grid. At this moment, of course, I couldn't conceive of any of that. I knew only that this chapter of my work was complete and that something interesting was bound to come next.

Exercise III

✦ Pulse Point Meditation

As you learn to identify pulse points, spend time with as many of them as you can, in repeated visits over weeks or months. In time, you will notice that some nodes are stronger than others.

1. Choose a pulse point and sit down in a comfortable spot. Begin a meditation by becoming aware of energy from the earth and sky entering your body and meeting in your heart or lower abdomen. Radiate love from your body into the land beneath you. Feel the loving energy expand from the pulse point beneath you into the surrounding landscape—like a wave moving out in all directions.

2. Tune in to the energy at this pulse point and understand that it has an intelligent awareness. As you did with the tree, greet this energy and ask to be shown some of its experience. Ask the land, "How are you today?"

3. Allow your body and mind to notice incoming sensations and images. You may notice particular aspects of your environment— like the rich smell of damp earth or the sounds of a nearby lawn mower, or you may have an overall emotional impression—of calm or joy or weariness. Observe as much as you can, without interpreting or explaining.

4. Gently ask the land about the beings that make up its community; try to gather information about the trees and animals, as well as the insects, grasses, and humans who dwell here or visit from time to time. There may be ancestral people connected to this land who watch over it. If you sense them, greet them with respect and openness.

5. Ask if there is a particular organism that governs this landscape—a grandfather or grandmother tree, or a rock or body of water who speaks for the whole? If yes, try to identify the specific organism and greet it, also, with respect. You may wish to dialog with this grandparent to learn more about the land's natural history.

6. Maintaining your meditative state, slowly open your eyes and try to see your surroundings from the point of view of its inhabitants, guardians, and spirits. You may wish to mentally scan the landscape through their eyes, or you may wish to walk around and perceive the land with deeper levels of understanding.

   In this process you may learn bits of history of the place, learn the plants that naturally abide here, or perceive imbalances of many kinds. As you look or move around the landscape you may also notice energy shifts—areas that feel secluded and private, for instance, versus those that are open and exposed. Some sections may seem exceptionally peaceful, while others may feel sad, overgrown, or even chaotic. Note these differences without trying to explain or understand them; being aware is the important part. Whichever way you choose to explore, make note of any areas that feel disturbed or unsettled.

7. Embrace a deep awareness of the interconnectedness of all the sights, sounds, movements, and energies. Appreciate the whole territory as a unity.

8. Slowly bring your awareness back into your own body, appreciating it, too, as a multidimensional community. Recognize the landscape as a reflection of your own being, and your own cells as mirrors of the land. Give thanks for the loving energy that cycles between you.

PART IV

The Healing

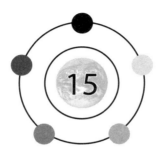

Into Darkness

In the days that followed the construction of our stone circle, I buzzed with excitement, hoping to discern some change in the world around me. I expected something big to happen, though I didn't know what. I found myself checking a website that monitors earthquake activity in the region. There wasn't anything significant, but I kept checking anyway.

I also read the web pages of various close–Indian Point campaigns, alert for any political or legal developments, but none appeared. I looked at the weather, the people around me, the newspaper—searching everywhere for some palpable sign that the region was responding to our work—but found nothing remarkable anywhere. After a day or two of this, I felt a deep exhaustion seeping into my bones. My head began to hurt, and I was listless and weepy.

"I guess building that stone circle was more exhausting than I realized," I told myself. "Better get some rest and stop looking at all those websites." But no amount of rest was enough, and I felt worse each day than I had the day before. Still, it wasn't until I was wincing each time I turned on a light that I recognized these symptoms as a return of Lyme disease. Sensitivity to light had been one of the stranger symptoms of my earlier illness, so its reappearance was a clear indication.

I had finished my antibiotic prescription about a week ago—just a day or two before the stone circle; that was unfortunate timing. The continuous excitement and exhaustion of those few days must have been a perfect breeding ground for any bacteria still alive in my body. Now I was backsliding and needed to start my healing from scratch again. I needed more antibiotics.

I had a hard time convincing my doctor of this, however. He was firmly in the camp of physicians who believed that three to four weeks of antibiotics would get rid of Lyme. "If you still feel sick after that, it must be something else," he told me over the phone when I asked for a refill of the prescription. I knew that there were alternate points of view about Lyme—some patients stayed on antibiotics for six weeks or even six months, some for even longer. As for me, I had the same specific and unusual symptoms that I'd had a month ago when I had been clearly diagnosed; I was sure I still had Lyme. But I wanted to be a good patient, and I wanted to be open to this doctor's wisdom.

"Something else like what?" I asked, genuinely hoping that he would have some ideas.

"Well," he answered after a moment. "You could have MS. Or a brain tumor."

Even in my weakened state I knew that this was very unlikely—and that it was bad medicine. What was a clear case of Lyme disease a month ago was most likely still Lyme disease. And even if he had some good reason to suspect that I had something more serious, it was irresponsible to suggest those terminal diseases over the telephone, without any evidence or preparation. "Please," I begged, not wanting my voice to reveal that I was angry, now, at what sounded like fearmongering. "Can I just try it for a few more weeks?"

After a while he agreed to give me two more weeks of doxycycline but made it clear that that would be the end of it. I thanked him and rushed off to the pharmacy to fill the prescription. In my heart, however, I had already decided that I would never go back to that doctor again. His willingness to deliberately scare me rather than talk to me openly was a behavior I couldn't work with. I'd have to find someone new. But I also realized that antibiotics were not going to be a miracle cure; if three weeks of medicine hadn't fixed me before, two weeks were not going to do it now. They would probably—I hoped—get me back on my feet, but what was I going to do after that?

The question of what would come later all but disappeared from my mind as the antibiotics began their work. I shivered with fever and twisted with pain. I felt like my spine had been replaced with iron. In a sweat of nausea and fatigue I began to worry about what the doctor had said. Maybe I did have a brain tumor or MS. I had certainly never felt so ill.

For a few days I just spun in a delirium of sickness and panic. My heart raced, my head and spine hurt, I couldn't sleep, and my brain kept running the same song loop over and over again. I didn't want to have a brain tumor, but the truth was that at the moment I would have been glad to be lying in a hospital bed, having other people take care of me. I wondered if perhaps I should go to a hospital, but the thought of having to get there was too exhausting. I lay back on the couch and decided not to think about it.

Luckily, modern medicine does work miracles sometimes, and the next day I began to feel better. Nowhere near good, but better enough to remember that I had to come up with a plan—I had ten days of medicine left.

I staggered into James's acupuncture office, hoping a treatment would help me pull myself together. Listing my complaints from head to toe, I felt completely unable to make any sense or coherent picture out of it. I knew that the sum total of my symptoms was inadequate to describe my experience. Something bigger and deeper was going on in my body than this litany of ailments. Only eight days ago I had been the magician of Dunderberg, and now I was a total wreck—fried from the inside out. "I feel as though I put my finger into a giant electric socket and completely blew my circuits," I told James, trying to put my feelings into words.

James kindly pointed out that that's exactly what I *had* done. "You basically stuck your whole body into the circuitry of the planet when we built that stone circle," he said. "You probably did fry a few transmission lines."

I thought about that for a few minutes. When I perform acupuncture on a client, I do feel like I'm plugging into an electrical network in his body. The qi that moves through the client—and through the needles to my hand—is a kinetic force, light and fast and powerful. During a treatment I am always aware of that force and direct it intentionally to where it is needed. If I don't maintain my awareness—if I am tired or distracted—then I can end up exhausted, or depressed, or, quite strangely, afflicted with the exact symptom I was trying to treat in the client.

As a practitioner, you learn these truths pretty quickly or you burn yourself out. Yet I had forgotten this basic dynamic during the building of the stone circle. I had failed to pay attention to the qi itself, and to my body's boundaries in regard to that qi. Some of it had clearly backfired, and I had blown my circuits. No wonder I felt so lousy. I looked up at James and nodded my understanding.

"Okay," he said thoughtfully. "Let me see if I can help shift that feeling, so you have a bit more energy available to bring to your healing." I asked James to avoid putting any needles in my head, as it was too sensitive right now, but to work along my spine and sacrum, which continued to feel stiff and painful. I lay on the treatment table, and he began to insert the needles. The moments of deep contact—when the qi "grabs" the needle, as we say in acupuncture—felt exactly right, and I began to relax with relief.

James dimmed the lights and left the room, leaving me to sink into the treatment. During an acupuncture session, clients usually drift into a kind of sleep—an "acu-sleep," as one of my teachers called it. Unlike a normal nap, this sleep is a profound state: a deep meditation in which our thoughts remain active, but our habits of mind and conceptions of self tend to relax a bit. We can reconnect with a deeper level of being—a part of ourselves that is pure potential. When we awaken at the end of a session, we surface from a place of peace with a renewed sense of possibility.

Today, as my treatment began, I found myself becoming gradually less focused on the specific areas of pain, and more aware of my body as a whole. I saw myself lying there in repose, like a chain of mountains, while inside my body bristled with life. "I am a landscape," I whispered to myself, identifying the hills and valleys of my torso. "And a river," I suddenly realized, as I saw my spine rippling through that landscape, carrying energy back and forth between my brain and my nervous system in an endless loop of connectivity that echoed the Hudson's tides.

"I am the Hudson!" I recognized with wonder, suddenly aware of the top and bottom of my spine, which neatly echoed the source and mouth of the Hudson. The source—where spinal cord meets brain—is like Moheakantuk's source in the high mountain lake. The mouth of my inner river was my sacrum, analogous to the Hudson's wide delta at the Atlantic Ocean. In between, the river of my spinal cord coursed through my body, its three ecosystems marked by my cervical, thoracic, and lumbar vertebrae.

In my mind's eye, I could see that my inner Hudson was ill just like the outer one; my swollen meninges were like the banks and bed of the river, inflamed by the tiny bacteria that cause Lyme. These bacteria shed toxins that sickened the whole of my inner river with poisons as invisible and insidious as radiation from the nuclear power plant.

"I need to help the river heal," I murmured as I drifted off, images of a healer at the riverside weaving through my mind: offerings made, vows undertaken, river merging into river, self dissolving into emptiness. . . .

The soft click of the doorknob pulled me back to awareness as James came in and began to remove the needles. "Wait till you hear this," I said to him as he finished his work. I sat up excitedly and explained my understanding of my spine as the Hudson, and my twin tasks of healing myself and the river as one and the same.

"That makes sense," James responded when I had finished. "The microcosm is the macrocosm—that's what we've been learning all along." He was right. For the past nine months, we had been continuously surprised to find the Earth mirroring the acupuncture body and responding to Chinese medicine. Now the hall of mirrors had revealed another layer; we were back to seeking healing on a human scale. It just so happened that I was the human.

At work the next day, nearly every client seemed to have a back problem, so I was palpating spines and working with that river of energy for most of the day. In Chinese medicine, the energy of the spine is shaped by the Governing Vessel, which begins deep in the pelvis and runs up the center of the spine. It is the partner of the Conception Vessel on the front of the body. Together they form a loop—the first circuit of energy that arises in the embryo after conception.

The Governing Vessel is our first experience of yang—the very beginning of our growth and the force that later compels us to pick up our heads and face the world. In this sense it is the kernel of relationship—that which prompts us to reach out.

As I was pondering this primal yang during my last session of the day, the electricity went out. It was the middle of August, so I imagined that extra demand from everyone's air conditioners had caused a blackout, as sometimes happens. However, one of the side benefits of practicing Iron Age medicine is that modern necessities like electricity don't play much of a role; as long as there's enough light in the room for me to get around without bumping into the furniture, I can work in a power outage as easily as anywhere. The treatment room got a little warm without the fan going, but other than that the lack of electricity was of little note.

In the car after my sessions I flicked on the radio and heard nothing but static. At station after station it was the same. I began to panic; were we under attack again? This was metro New York, where the radio dial is usually crammed so full of music and talk that you can't find static even if you want it. I ran back inside to make a few phone calls, pressing the keypad with shaking fingers.

A local innkeeper reassured me that he hadn't heard anything about terrorism, though he had heard on his police scanner that the entire Northeast was blacked out—from New York up into parts of Canada. Yikes.

With the worst of my fears eased, I began to take stock. Given the extent of the damage, the blackout was likely to last for several days; I had to be sure I had enough food and water to tide me over. The refrigerator would become a problem pretty fast, as would my plumbing, but I had lots of bottled water, nonperishable food, and a gas stove that would work just fine without power. Out in the country, power cuts are pretty common, so we learn to be prepared. We also learn that blackouts have their beauty.

There is something inherently soothing about the blanket of stillness that descends during a power outage: no refrigerator or power lines humming, no vibrating machines or buzzing appliances, no glowing lights from the omnipresent digital clocks and consoles. Yet I hear so many insects, and leaves whispering in the breeze, animals rustling, and a subtle rhythmic whoooosh that makes me imagine the land itself is breathing softly, like a sleeping child. I know that there are still diesel engines running somewhere, and cars, and backup generators in crucial places like hospitals and grocery stores and nuclear power plants, but the soundscape here is peaceful.

As night fell, it fell hard, covering everything with a totality I had never seen before. Without the glow of Manhattan and its densely populated suburbs, the night sky revealed itself to be its own source of light. There were so many stars that they actually lit the sky, instead of hanging like dim bulbs that I had to search for. The Milky Way was a dense white river—an unmistakable path that suddenly brought ancient mythology to life; I understood for the first time why people have been telling stories about the stars for hundreds and thousands of years.

The telephone rang, and I jumped with surprise, pulled from my night journey back into the modern world, where I always keep an old-fashioned phone plugged into a jack so that I am not completely cut off when the power goes out. Sometimes a big storm can knock out the phone lines, too, though that is a rare occurrence.

"Hello?" I said expectantly, glad that someone had made the effort to reach toward me through the darkness.

"Did you have something to do with this blackout, you crazy priestess of light?" my friend Tina cackled into the phone. "What did you do?"

"I really don't know," I answered slowly, surprised that my friend the Western physician had been the one to verbalize the thought I hadn't dared to acknowledge. It had been only ten days since we'd built the stone circle. "Do you think it's possible?"

"I don't know either," Tina answered, still laughing with delight. "There's so much power circulating around in the Earth and our bodies and the electrical grid, and so much we don't understand about our interconnectedness with all of it—maybe you really did find a junction point between them. That's kind of the way acupuncture works, isn't it?"

Not for the first time, Tina's lightning-fast assessment of the situation left me breathless. That *is* the way acupuncture works; we just don't usually expect it to work so . . . big. If this was a response to our work on Dunderberg, it was a much larger response than I would have thought possible—or desirable. Maybe we had gotten in over our heads and had messed with forces way out of our control.

The blackout was most likely just a coincidence. Later analysis would reveal that it had actually begun in Ohio, then spread eastward. In truth, though, we would never know whether our stone circle had had anything to do with the blackout or not. We could imagine that it had, or imagine that it hadn't, but in either case it would be only our imaginations telling the story. No deeper truth was accessible here.

Once I admitted that it was pointless to try to figure out what had caused the blackout, I was able to think about it more creatively. I wondered how the landscape would be affected; would the darkness be good or bad for the river, and for Dunderberg?

Well, with no electricity, there'd be less human activity, less pollution, and less noise—less stress from every source in the whole landscape. I imagined Dunderberg surveying the primeval darkness that stretched for mile after mile, remembering what it felt like to be the most powerful being in the region. Maybe the mountain could only truly awaken when the modern monsters around it were all asleep.

I hoped that the river, also, could take a kind of nap and accomplish some essential healing in the darkness. Not that the river would stop running, of course, or stop changing with the tides, but maybe it could just rest—whatever that might mean for a river. "Oh!" I suddenly shouted out loud in my dark and silent house. "This is the river's acu-sleep!" After our stone circle acupuncture, the river was having its rest. I thought about the revelations I'd experienced during my most recent treatment—my body as a landscape, my spine as the river: Would the river now dream that it was me?

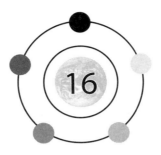

The Great Turning

The vision of my spine as the river stuck with me. Somehow this image gave me hope, and I clung to it without knowing exactly why it felt so important. Of course, I knew that in Western medicine, the idea that my body or my illness could reflect something external like the landscape would be considered crazy; my illness was certainly caused by bacteria, and any suggestion that it had some spiritual link to a river would sound, to a doctor, like mental illness. But I had stepped outside the boundaries of Western medicine a long time ago and was used to spilling out of its diagnostic framework. I'd found the flexible, symbolic, poetic systems of Eastern medicine to be very welcoming in contrast. Now, however, I had stretched even those beyond recognition.

There was no model in Chinese medicine for this doubling back of the disease onto me; Chinese doctors are supposed to help the patient heal, not become sick themselves. In this light, I would be considered a poor doctor indeed. Still, I believed that there was something in this experience that was neither failure nor mental illness. When I saw my spine as the river, it was lit up and glowing—like a cartoon lightbulb saying, "Bright idea!" There had to be some other meaning in it.

To find that meaning, I needed to look outside of both Western medicine and Chinese medicine, because I had become something other than an acupuncturist when I had planted stones into the skin of the Earth. In employing the most ancient tools—the very elements of earth and stone—and in accepting my visions as legitimate parts of the medicine, I was more like a shaman or a priestess: a medicine woman of an older order. I had reentered the primal relationship of humankind with creation, reawakening the ability to communicate directly with the spiritual intelligences of the Earth.

I knew that in many shamanic traditions, healers often take on the illnesses of their patients as a part of the cure. The illness is understood to be the reflection of a problem that may cross several social and spiritual realms at once and can be treated in any or all of those realms. As the shaman works to heal herself with the multidimensional tools that are available to her, she may bring about simultaneous change in the world around her, altering the diseased aspects of the patient, the community, the ancestors, and so on, that led to the illness in the first place.

If this was my model, Lyme disease was a comprehensible stage of the treatment—I had effectively linked myself with the river and was manifesting its ailments. Of course, I understood that the river didn't actually have Lyme disease, and that I did not suffer from radiation or thermal pollution, yet the surface parallels of our problems were enough to establish a connection in my view. Both illnesses were caused by pernicious, invisible entities—*Borrelia burgdorferi* bacteria in my case, radioactive atoms in the case of the river—that caused systemic, cumulative, and unpredictable damage. In both cases, the battle against an invisible enemy felt mytho-poetic; I could easily imagine a supernatural realm where these two experiences were conjoined. The question was, what I was going to do about it. How was I going to accomplish the next stage of the treatment and get myself better?

In this old-order medicine, I didn't have a clear sense of what the next steps were supposed to be. Typically, healers are trained within a specific tradition, and their treatment strategies are drawn from the tools of their training. But I had scrambled several traditions together, then invented a few of my own; in trying to treat Moheakantuk and myself in relationship to each other, I was working without a map. It was both exhilarating and daunting.

One day, however, I realized that there was a modern context emerging for the kind of medicine I was doing: the fields of Deep Ecology and the closely related Spiritual Ecology were new movements that recognized that every living being has intrinsic value, regardless of whether or not they are "useful" to humans.[1] Steeped in the wisdom of indigenous people around the globe, these new disciplines recognized the spirited animacy of the entire living world, as well as the urgent need for the human parts of the Earth community to acknowledge that animacy so that we stop destroying it. The survival of our planet, including our own species, hangs in the balance.

In recent years, the cosmic activist Thomas Berry had published two groundbreaking books, *The Dream of the Earth* and *The Great Work,* in which he forthrightly spelled out the necessity of transitioning "from a period of human devastation of the Earth to a period when humans would be present to the planet . . ."[2] What Berry called the "Great Work," the eco-philosopher Joanna Macy called the "Great Turning." Both describe the same thing: turning our civilization from one of destruction to one that will benefit the Earth and its beings.

The mechanics of that turning will need to be manifold and widespread. Both Macy and Berry lay out plans for changing our relationship to the Earth at many levels, describing legal, political, and environmental structures that our civilization needs to re-create from the ground up. Both writers acknowledge that such transition can happen only as individuals begin to transform themselves and their own relationships to nature; it is the quality of relationship that is at issue.

"The most remarkable feature of this historical moment on Earth," says Joanna Macy, "is not that we are on the way to destroying the world—we've actually been on the way for quite a while. It is that we are beginning to wake up, as from a millennia-long sleep, to a whole new relationship to our world, to ourselves, and each other."[3] One of Macy's contributions to the forming of those new relationships is a ritual she calls a "Council of All Beings," in which human participants take on the character of nonhuman beings—of dolphins or elm trees or rivers, and the like—and speak to one another in an attempt to deepen their understanding of the experience of these beings.

Thomas Berry, too, offers conversation with the natural world as a remedy for our ills. "We are talking only to ourselves," Berry writes. "We are not talking to the rivers, we are not listening to the wind and stars. We have broken the great conversation. By breaking that conversation we have shattered the universe. All the disasters that are happening now are a consequence of that spiritual 'autism.'"[4]

I felt certain that I had broken through that spiritual autism in my work with Moheakantuk and Dunderberg; having been in deep conversation with both of them for many months, I honored them as beings in their own right. What was new to me in these writings, however, was the global imperative they described. While I had begun this journey with a very personal goal—that of helping Moheakantuk to heal—and had followed a creative, spontaneously evolving path in my efforts to achieve that goal, I was unknowingly a part of a much larger movement.

The Great Turning/Great Work showed me that my individualized dream was really a part of a universal story. It was part of the shared experience in which we humans are learning to reinvent ourselves and our relationship to the community of life. I was following the call that came to me, but other people were certainly hearing their own such calls, and answering in the ways that they knew how.

This was the Great Work that Berry referred to—the work of every being following its own highest calling as we turn the great boat of human civilization in an entirely new direction. Having my work, and my entire approach to the natural world, described and so deeply validated by these great thinkers anchored me in a way I didn't know I needed. Feeling part of a larger context—the context of necessary global shift—erased my feelings of uncertainty and showed me that my work was entirely real and also important. This project mattered.

And if the project mattered, then I did, too. I was an integral part of this story, and as such I needed to keep participating. The fact that I was still so ill told me that the project wasn't finished yet; the locus of action had simply shifted (temporarily, I hoped) from the landscape to my own body.

Writings about the Great Turning didn't offer many clues about personal healing, however; the only evidence I could find of the connection between personal and planetary health was this, from ecopsychologist Theodore Roszak: "It may well be that more and more of what people bring before doctors and therapists for treatment—agonies of body and spirit—are symptoms of the biospheric emergency registering at the most intimate level of life. The Earth hurts, and we hurt with it."[5]

I did feel that my illness was, at least in part, a symptom of the "biospheric emergency," but I wasn't quite sure where to turn for treatment. The straightforward path of antibiotics was not available to me right now; I might be able to find a different doctor who would prescribe them, but that would take some time. In the meantime, I needed something else—something that was capable of healing both me and Moheakantuk.

I made a list of all the health practitioners I had met or heard of who might be able to help me. When I'd finished, I had a list of thirteen people, including medical doctors, herbalists, psychics, homeopaths, and spiritual healers. I vowed to call them one by one over the next several days. I was exhausted from all of this thinking, but somehow hopeful, too. This list was the first proactive thing I'd been able to do to challenge my illness.

That night I had a dream that rewrote my healing challenge in strangely fairy-tale terms and showed me a way forward:

I was waiting in a line to see a famous spiritual healer, who was consulting with clients inside a bejeweled tent. Those of us in line were instructed to do two things while we each waited our turn. First, we were to think of a question—one question only—that we would be able to ask the healer. Second, we were to pick a talisman from one of several trays and boxes arrayed on tables in front of us. We would keep this talisman with us until we were healed.

I went over to the table and began to look through the trays, which were strewn with all kinds of pretty things—crystals and polished stones; animal figurines; miniature goddesses and gods from many different religions; carved wands and other geometrical forms; coins in gold, silver, and copper. I worried that I would have a hard time choosing among all those treasures, but as I looked more closely I found that some were immediately more interesting to me than others. In a few minutes I had chosen a walnut-sized flattened oval, which seemed to be made out of pearl, although it was much larger and flatter than any real pearl I'd ever seen. It was backed with a heavy green stone and had a solid heft in my hand.

Holding this pearly talisman in my hand, I began to think of my question. "How can I get better?" came to mind, but I was afraid that it sounded too passive. I knew this journey would require some work of me, and I needed to acknowledge that in my question. "What do I need to do?" might get me some specifics, but they might not be related to healing from this disease. As an assistant led me into the tent, my knees were shaking. I was shown to a low cushioned stool, where I sat in front of the healer, both of us silent for a few minutes.

"What is your question, dear?" she asked in a kindly singsong voice. Unsteadily, I reached for the words I had planned, glad I had taken the time to formulate them carefully, hoping they would garner me the information I needed.

"What do I need to do to help myself heal?" I asked.

The healer was silent for a moment. Then her face lit up with a smile. "You need to play chess!" she said brightly.

I awoke with that puzzling answer echoing through my mind—grasping in vain for my talisman and trying to interpret this disappointing advice. I knew in a deep way that the answer was a real answer; if I could figure out how to "play chess" as instructed, I would get better. I just didn't know what that meant. This was a story world again, and it was speaking to me in symbolism instead of concrete instruction. "Play

chess?" Not literally, surely. Chess would challenge my mental facul-
ties, but I couldn't see any way that it would physically heal my body.
Yet chess is a metaphor for other challenges—most famously in *Alice
in Wonderland,* but in many other stories as well. I looked up *chess* in a
dictionary of symbolism and read that "games in general are symbolic
of the patterns of life—with chequered patterns referring to chequered
careers, of dark episodes alternating with light, ups with downs. . . . The
different conflicting forces move, inter-relate, lock, and fly apart."[6]

I didn't like the sound of that—locking and flying apart sounded
way too intense. Yet chess is, famously, a crucible of a game; each turn
demands your full attention and your very best move, and the whole
state of play can be transformed in an instant. Applied to my healing, I
interpreted this to mean that I was looking at a path of ups and downs,
of strategy and concentration, and intense relationship. It seemed that I
would not be able to simply pick a cure and watch it work; I would have
to take it step by step. This was sounding like a long and demanding
process, and it was *not* what I wanted to hear.

Still, the dream reminded me that real healing *is* a process, not
a one-step cure. I knew this intimately from the practice of Chinese
medicine, yet I had been wishing for something faster and easier when
it came to this battle with Lyme. Now I had to let go of the wishful
thinking and deal with reality—I had to play chess, one move at a time.

My first move in the chess game was to turn to the list of practitioners
I had made the previous day. Wanting, first of all, strong herbs to take the
place of antibiotics, I booked an appointment with Dr. Susan, an herbalist
in Chinatown. The trip to Dr. Susan's office—requiring car, train, subway, and foot travel—was exhausting, and by the time I got there I was so
spent that I sank into a chair and cried. Dr. Susan waited, then motioned
for me to extend my wrists so she could listen to my pulses.

After a few minutes of silence she nodded her head, as if she were
beginning to understand something. "Oh, you're very depleted," she
said gently. "Your Spleen Qi is very weak, and Kidney Qi too. What
happened?"

I told her briefly about Lyme disease, and antibiotics, and the resurgence of the symptoms.

"Yes, yes," she nodded. "Antibiotics will weaken the disease, but they weaken you, too. Now you need to strengthen yourself before you can focus on attacking the bacteria again." She wrote down a formula for me, and I waited in the large, fragrant, old-fashioned pharmacy as the pharmacists filled the prescription. The smell of raw Chinese herbs is cloying, but also deeply comforting, because it promises relief. I thought about Dr. Susan's words: I certainly did need herbs to strengthen me and was looking forward to starting the prescription. For the second time in days, I began to feel hopeful; maybe I would be able to get better after all.

I watched as the pharmacists opened drawer after wooden drawer in a shelf that lined the whole back wall of the pharmacy. They pulled out handfuls of leaves and sticks and resins and seeds, weighed each ingredient in a handheld balance scale, and distributed it onto a row of plates waiting on the counter. This was Chinese herbal medicine, practiced as it has been for thousands of years. When they were finished, the contents of six plates were poured into six bags, and I was given the instructions for boiling them and drinking the resulting tea. This was not shamanic medicine, exactly—traditional Chinese herbalism is a very rational, empirical system of medicine—but it *was* medicine from the earth. That made it a link between all of my worlds; it was both magical and ordinary, and I had a sense that it was just what I needed.

On the journey home, I thought about how weak I had become and wondered why I had waited so long to get herbs. If I were going to accept the idea that my illness reflected the illness of the Earth, then I had to understand that the process of healing myself was part of my vow to help the Hudson. *I was bound* to do as good a job of recovering as I could. Not that I wouldn't be trying my best in any case, but the sense of obligation changed my perspective. Instead of passively waiting for one doctor or another to cure me, I was suddenly the one in charge. I had to keep seeking until I reached a good result.

Over time I discovered that this switch from passive to active went quite deep. Approaching my healing as a vow I had made to another being gave me a determination that was unfamiliar. It turned me from feeling like a difficult patient into an advocate and gave me permission to be headstrong. Somehow, I now felt that I was obliged to pursue unconventional therapies in the quest to find out what worked, and equally obliged to reject some conventional ones that didn't. I eagerly experimented with herbs and supplements I'd never even heard of before but didn't think twice about throwing a prescription for antidepressants into the trash. This was part of playing chess: quickly discarding moves that didn't serve my long-term strategy of getting better.

I decided that for each aspect of my personal healing journey, I would try to imagine some appropriate correlate for the river. When I boiled and drank these Chinese herbs, I would imagine the whole ecosystem of the river growing stronger—healthy plants and wildlife increasing as destructive ones shrank away. As the inflammation in my spine began to recede, I would visualize the water becoming cooler and cleaner, the banks and bed of the river becoming less polluted—eliminating the excess heat and toxins. Deciding when to strengthen weaknesses and when to eliminate excess—another fundamental aspect of Chinese medicine—would become another part of the step-by-step healing that my chess dream had described.

As I drank my first dose of herbs that evening, I felt grateful to Dr. Susan for having recognized and addressed my body's weakness. I also, unexpectedly, felt grateful to my body for *being* the river—for letting me experience something like what the river was going through. In learning how to treat my own symptoms, I would be able to take my medicine for Moheakantuk to a deeper level.

Admitting that I felt grateful to my body for the Lyme disease that was making me so miserable was quite a shock. Being sick was bad, and some part of me believed I should be angry with my body—and angry at the landscape that had furnished the ticks—for failing me. But I did not feel anger.

Instead, an inner wisdom reminded me that my body is not simply a vehicle for my amusement, successful when I am well and failing me when I'm ill. Rather, my body is serving as an instrument of growth, inviting me to become a deeper human being who is more connected to the rest of the living world. Right now my body was illustrating a story of the hardship and suffering that were endemic to this place. As I fought to regain my health in tenuous steps, I would be writing the next chapters of that story for myself and for the Hudson River valley.

In choosing to feel gratitude instead of anger at this process, I was stepping outside of the warrior model of medicine, which fights disease and tries to eliminate it. Instead I was learning from my disease, recognizing it as a part of me that offered clues about ways I could grow, and ways I could help to heal the river. Certainly I still needed to kill off the bacteria, but I could do it without hating them, or hating myself for being ill.

And this attitude, I realized, was inherently strengthening. Feeling thankful to my body and connected by it to the landscape were palpable strengths. I still felt sick, but differently now. Aware that my job was to grow, rather than simply to fight, I could see even the illness as having a place in my life.

With that conviction, everything changed. The turning of a miserable disease into a seed of my future was a transformative shock that cleared away my confusion and self-pity about being ill. In their place was a clear and creative space that left room for me to begin my healing.

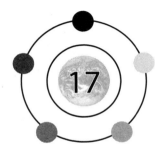

Healing/Reconceived

Working with the doctors and healers and supplements I had envisioned for myself, I slowly improved in fits and starts. Sometimes a promising treatment backfired, or some unanticipated stress overwhelmed my system, and I would be sick again for days or weeks at a time. It was a hard game of chess indeed, against an invisible but very powerful opponent. Nevertheless, I did grow stronger as time went by.

One weekend, I traveled up to Vermont to learn more about Patrick's kind of earth acupuncture. He had kindly agreed to have me tag along as he worked on a property whose owners had hired him because the well seemed to be drying up. They didn't know if they needed to drill a new well, or if something could be done to save the old one.

At the front boundary of the property, we each took a moment to greet the land in our own way. I had forgotten to bring cornmeal with me but smiled inwardly to the ancestors and guardians of this place. Offering love and respect, I promised to listen with an open heart to whatever the land had to say.

When Patrick had finished his whispered dialogue with the beings of the land, he led me toward the well. As we walked, he eyed the surrounding landscape and asked if I detected any areas of stagnant energy. He began to shuffle his feet along the ground as if he were wading through a shin-deep puddle, though I could see only air. "I'm feeling a very yin and stuck current right here," he motioned toward the ground, "and a kind of emptiness off to the side of it."

I concentrated on my breathing and cleared my thoughts as I had when I listened to the river's pulses. I didn't think a full pulse taking was necessary here, but I wanted to tune in with this landscape and learn something about it. With my eyes open but unfocused, I found I could "see" the energy of the land as I do a body: some areas looked constricted, and my breathing tightened as I scanned them; others seemed to draw me toward them, or to spiral around in confusion.

I walked toward Patrick and found him standing beside a spot where the energy pooled and then seemed to disappear. "Right here?" I asked him, as I pointed toward the pool of energy. He nodded and pulled a small cloth bag from his backpack, from which he drew two short rods—each about the length of a pencil, though thinner.

"Let's try copper first," he said, and handed me the rod, as he had handed me the engineering flag that day on Dunderberg. Once again, I was struck by Patrick's generosity: his willingness to step away from the limelight so I could move into it was so unusual that it reconfigured something in me instantaneously. I felt confident and strong. I squatted down, remembering the way my colleagues had gathered around me on the mountain to help me find the center point of our stone circle. How charged that moment had been, and how calm this one was; would I still be able to do it?

I scanned the earth with my left hand, feeling the eddies of swirling qi. When I found the tightest point, I inhaled and inserted the copper needle, eyeing the spot a few inches away where the energy seemed to disappear. With my right hand holding the needle, I slowly began to manipulate it, feeling my way around under the surface of the ground. It felt just like needling a person! In my mind's eye I saw a grid appear underground—like a large fabric netting that reached to the horizon and beyond. I saw that there were several such grids layered beneath the surface of the earth and understood that I was to direct my needle toward one in particular, which was a forest-green color. I pecked lightly at the green netting with my needle, angling and reaching to aim for the pinpoint place where the energy seemed the most stuck.

I perform these same actions every day when I work on people, but I had rarely had this kind of visual accompaniment. I watched in fascination as the netting rippled like an ocean wave, sending the impulse through the whole grid. In a moment the "empty" place of no energy had opened, and a wave rolled into it like a river whose dam has been released.

"That was nice and quick," said Patrick beside me. I looked up and saw him smiling broadly. "I knew you'd be good at this."

"Did you see it too?" I asked. "Did you see that grid? And did you see the energy rolling in?" Patrick explained that his experience was different from mine. He largely felt the energy by its temperature—cold yin energy pooling around his ankles, hot yang floating up around his eyes—although sometimes he saw flashes of light and shadow as well.

"From what I have seen," he continued, "the land tends to speak to us in whatever language we are likely to understand. So you might listen to pulses and see visions, Ivan hears stones singing, I feel currents of energy and talk to the spirits of the landscape. Our job is simply to listen and respond to the best of our ability. The fact of communication is more important than the method."

Back at home, I continued to experiment with the landscape. I discovered that not every piece of land wanted or needed acupuncture; some areas just wanted to be cleared of litter, others asked for stone cairns or wildflowers. A few places really just wanted to be acknowledged. Over time, I realized that a willingness to listen was the most important thing, and that a gentle way of communicating that willingness was also necessary. Just as we say "Hi," or "How are you?" when we greet a person, it is important to similarly greet trees and mountains and other elements of the landscape if you want to be open to relationship.

For me, breathing deeply turned out to be a vital prelude to any kind of communication with a nonhuman intelligence; it helped me focus my attention, silence the internal chatter, and tune in to the subtle energies around me. In addition, I liked to make an offering of some kind—cornmeal or nuts or even a hair from my head if nothing else was available. Along with this offering, I would give thanks to the being I was hoping to communicate with—tree or flower or bird—for all that they contribute to the landscape and its inhabitants.

Other land healers I met offered songs or dances, or flower essences, or prayers as ways to get a conversation going. But some form of acknowledgement and attention was a universal theme for those working with nature. "The Earth needs our attention," writes the Sufi mystic Llewellyn Vaughan-Lee. "It needs us to help heal its body, damaged by our exploitation, and also its soul, wounded by our desecration, our forgetfulness of its sacred nature."[1]

As I became a better listener to the landscape, I became a better listener overall. I found I was hearing more details from my clients, understanding my friends and family more deeply, and also perceiving the ups and downs of my own healing more clearly than I had before. When my friends Sarah and Jerry visited in November and asked to see the stone circle, the timing felt right. I decided to go back to the mountain to find out what, if anything, it would say to me now.

We began at Jones Point, then walked up the Dunderberg trail. It was a pleasant hike in the fall leaves, but I was bewildered at how undramatic the whole scene was. Even the view from Jones Point had not seemed very threatening—just ugly. Either the land was still deeply asleep, or I was really broken—I could not get a ping or blip or an inkling of presence beyond that of myself and my friends. By the time we reached the stone circle, I felt completely defeated: it was all but invisible. I wouldn't have noticed the stones at all if I wasn't looking for them.

I was hugely disappointed, and also kind of embarrassed: the work of my entire past year looked like nothing. I tried to explain this to Sarah and Jerry—the pain of the gulf between what I had felt then and what I saw now. They thoughtfully reminded me that this project had never been about creating something to look at. This circle was not intended as a monument or a work of public art—it was medicine, and medicine often works on invisible levels.

"Anyway," Sarah pointed out, "it does look like something—but something more out of reach than immediate. It is mysterious and cosmic, like a constellation." I liked the sound of that: a constellation upon the Earth—like a mirror for the stars. This was a virtual bridge between earth and sky—a link that might allow something new to grow. Looking around at the wind-tossed mountain, however, I didn't see a sign of anything new. On the contrary, everything looked as old as the hills; even the power plant appeared to be blending in with its surroundings somehow. I left the mountain feeling sad and uncertain; had all of my work amounted to nothing? Where was the evidence of change?

I spoke on the phone with Patrick, to see if he thought anything was changing. He dowsed the mountain and found it struggling. "Something in the midsection feels very sick," he said, in a pained voice. "Almost like a twisted gut, or something that needs to come out. Owww.

"The mountain is very uncomfortable," he continued, summing up his observations, "and needs time to work through this troubled energy. I don't recommend that you visit again for at least three months."

I didn't mind staying away from the mountain for a little while, but I did want to know if we had been successful in helping it to wake up. I wondered if the land and the river were beginning to heal, or if there was something more that I needed to do to fulfill my promise to Moheakantuk. I thought about Patrick's reaction, "like a twisted gut or something that needs to come out." Now his words made me think of the nut-brown mother as I had seen her on my first trip to Dunderberg—in labor. Maybe something new was being born *right now*.

The idea of conceiving something new had come up more than once in this project, but as with many aspects of the journey, I hadn't taken the idea literally. Now, however, the references to birth seemed so overwhelming that I was compelled to revisit the whole idea; I began to write down the images of birth that had appeared since the beginning of the stone circle project. Finding that I couldn't really separate the birth imagery from that of conception and DNA, I included those references in the list as well. Considered together, they made a significant list:

- The phallus shape of the Indian Point nuclear power plant
- The DNA letters carved into a tree on the Dunderberg trail
- The double-helix shape of the two round clearings
- The vision of the nut-brown mother in labor that I'd seen in my mind's eye the first time James and I had climbed Dunderberg Mountain
- Our identification of Moheakantuk as the Conception Vessel
- The newborn fawn that Ivan, Lucie, and I had encountered on the trail
- The crystals from Tintagel—the conception place of King Arthur—that Ivan had brought and planted at Dunderberg
- The vision of the double helix woven into the landscape that I'd seen after our work at Dunderberg and the Capuchin monastery
- The nine months that had elapsed from the time I'd decided to build a stone circle to the day that we had done it

The richness of this imagery went well beyond the cosmic task of merely suggesting conception and seemed to point clearly to a new birth coming from that conception. A new birth would certainly be an exciting result of my work, but I still wasn't sure what that could mean. There wasn't going to be a new river, or a new mountain, so . . . what could possibly be born?

To jump-start my thoughts, I began to research DNA, focusing on the events at conception. I learned that the DNA molecules of the sperm and the egg both multiply like crazy at conception. Each molecule splits itself down the middle, into two distinct and identical halves that both contain an exact replica of the genes of the whole that it came from. Next, the separated halves of the sperm's DNA each connect with one half of the egg's DNA, and they zip themselves together—a perfect gene splice—making the first cells of a completely new being. A poetic and biological mystery, DNA both multiplies and divides itself. It teaches us that the miracle of each new life comes of combining old information in new ways.

The individual formed from this process of union has never existed before and yet is indelibly composed of two preexisting wholes. And those previous people were themselves each made up of two distinct halves. And so on back through time, back to the DNA we share with the first human beings, and the apes, and even the fishes and plants. What we think of as defining our individuality is actually a part of every other living thing on the planet; our DNA contains snippets that are identical to sections of mouse DNA and rhododendron DNA and virus DNA and so on. Each individual's genome simply combines the available information in a unique way. Nowadays, geneticists are also discovering that some people's bodies actually contain more than one genotype of human DNA. These human chimeras are inescapable reminders that we all contain multitudes.

The fact that each new person's DNA is formed at conception was not news to me, but I suddenly understood it differently than I had before; now this sequence of events sounded very like the development of the Extraordinary Vessels according to Chinese medicine. Forming at conception and creating the blueprint that determines the development of the human being—this was an equally fitting description of DNA and the Conception Vessel.

Now I had the link I needed to understand how these ideas of conception and birth fit in with my work. If the Hudson was the Conception Vessel, it was like the DNA of the landscape that had formed around it. In this sense, Moheakantuk defined and governed the whole region—exactly as the art, literature, and anthropological history had been describing it for centuries. The ways that Indian Point was now changing the river were therefore a fundamental threat to the entire area; the organism of the landscape was being mutated at a genetic level. No wonder the river had been calling for help.

I discovered that Thomas Berry had been thinking about DNA as well. He suggested that humans need to re-create culture based on what our DNA needs, rather than what our current cultures tell us we need. He wrote, "We must go back to the genetic imperative from which human cultures emerge originally. . . . We must invent, or reinvent, a sustainable human culture by a descent into our pre-rational, our instinctive resources. . . . What is needed is not transcendence but 'inscendence,' not the brain but the gene."[2]

I liked to think that in some symbolic way, my work had been creating new DNA; reseeding the landscape and my own body with an integrated, inclusive blueprint that provided an image of how to grow into a healthier future. This idea appealed to me greatly—particularly the way it was drawing the most significant aspects of the whole project into an almost-coherent whole. But I still felt hazy about the specifics. If we had created a blueprint, or a new path forward, what was it, exactly?

The next few weeks were strange ones. I didn't feel quite done with the stone circle project but couldn't think of anything else to do for it, either. Like a partner pacing outside the delivery room, I was just waiting for that new baby—the new something that I believed was being born from our work. "Geologic time," I reminded myself. "This could take awhile."

In the early months of the new year, 2004, I began to feel that my work with the river was drawing to a close. Although I had not experienced any tangible conclusion to the stone circle story, I just wasn't thinking about it much anymore. Instead of feeling pulled southward toward the river, I was increasingly drawn north to Vermont—and to human-centered activities like writing and dating. I met a strong and gentle man and began to think seriously about leaving the Hudson Valley.

One day I realized with surprise that something deep had shifted; I was living my own life now, instead of the river's—spending my time doing whatever I wanted or needed, not what the river was calling for.

And it was a different life from the one I'd had a year ago, when I began the stone circle project—a much richer one. Where I used to feel lonely, I now felt in relationship with the whole world—with stars and trees, plants and mountains and birds, as well as with my very human boyfriend.

With the next breath, I suddenly understood that my renewed sense of relationship was itself a kind of parturition. My awareness of myself as part of the landscape, sharing common ancestors with all that stood, swam, walked, flew, crawled, and flowed, was actually a birth from the point of view of all those other beings. They now had a new relative: a new two-legged cousin who could listen and laugh with them, and sing and talk, and grieve.

Each time a person awakens to this primary relationship with the land, he is a new arrival in the family of life—one who can participate in the community and contribute to its growth. This is a crucial step on the path to maturity. For we can't expect the gods "to look us in the face," writes C. S. Lewis, "'til we have faces"[3]—that is, until we present ourselves to the relationship with honesty and openness. Perhaps *I* was the birth I had been waiting for.

This was a sweet vision, and I laughed to think that the answer had been in me all along. But part of me also knew that this project wasn't just about me; it was about relationship, and relationship takes two. In order to be in real relationship with other consciousnesses, I had to acknowledge their ability—and their responsibility—to participate. This was the significance of the intertwining spiral of the DNA—the mutual twisting and turning around each other, like the continual back and forth of Moheakantuk's tides: we give and take, we listen and respond, we acknowledge the divinity of the other, and recognize that our own divinity is thus revealed.

The new birth was therefore an "us": an awakening to the multidimensional awareness that is the consciousness of creation. Of course, mystics and healers and indigenous people have never lost touch with this rich awareness, even as it disappeared from the experience of

Western life. In recent years, however, many more beings have joined the effort to bring this awareness back into the ordinary world. Signs of the many new births thus engendered include new concepts, new vocabulary, and entirely new fields of learning that have arisen from our need to understand this notion of shared planetary awareness.

Fields like Spiritual Ecology, Ecopsychology, and Earth Healing now join the age-old disciplines of indigenous cultures worldwide in understanding that we are aspects of the Earth's entirety: the organelles of her body, the sparks of her soul. Each of us is a single pulsating cell within her great heart, equal partners in the new creation. At the moment, our species is a cancer, destroying the body we are entirely dependent upon. But each person who awakens to the reality of shared consciousness with nature transforms instantly from a cancerous cell to a resplendently healthy one, becomes a functional part of the planet's life force and increases its chances for survival.

One by one we work to turn these living cells "on," bringing ourselves and our planetary being back to life. None of us knows where the tipping point is, but in time, with enough of us participating, we may reverse the decline and return to the work of living in harmony with the rest of creation. Then, when the gods are finally able to look us in the face, we will be able to look back, smiling.

Exercise IV

→ **Building a Stone Mandala to Balance Earth Energies**

To create a mandala, you will need a magnetic compass as well as natural materials like stones, sticks, sand, or dirt. Look for four stones that share similar colors, sizes, and shapes. Find a fifth stone that is different from the others to mark the center of your mandala. To add color, you can also include cornmeal, flour, nuts, seeds, or berries.

1. Connect with a pulse point as you did in the previous exercise. Make offerings and affirm your intention to nourish the land.

2. Ask if there is any disharmony you can help to correct. Scan with your mind and eyes to find a place that is turbid or sickly. You may see an area of stunted or deadened growth, experience an unpleasant smell of rotting, or find a place that simply feels confusing, causing your feelings to sink. Certain views may make you feel sad or afraid.

3. Ask the landscape if a mandala or other earthwork would be welcome at or near this turbid point. Wait for a response.

4. When you are ready to create a mandala, find a point that feels like a strong center. The center of your circle will connect with the piece of earth you're working with. Make a prayer to the earth and sky as you place your stone directly on this point. Sprinkle a little bit of cornmeal or other offering onto the stone as you give thanks for the opportunity to bring healing energy to this place. Mentally connect this stone to the heart of the landscape.

5. Hold your magnetic compass directly over the center stone, and find the north-pointing arrow. Place your compass on the ground just north of the center stone, so that the north axis is a clear line.

6. With your eyes on the center stone, visualize the north axis extending one to two feet outward. Select a spot along this line that feels like a good boundary; this will determine the circumference of your mandala.

7. Pick one of the four cornerstones to mark the north point. Hold it in your hand and let it symbolize all the growth that exists on the

skin of the Earth at this place and time: grasses, trees, rocks, water, animals, insects, humans, buildings, and the like. Place the stone along the north axis at the boundary point you have chosen, and sprinkle with an offering.

8. Now draw an imaginary line from the north stone through the center stone and down to the place that will be the south point. Make sure it is the same distance from the center as the north stone.

     Choose a stone for the south point and hold it in your hand, connecting it to all that lies below the ground at this point: roots, rocks, earth, seeds, worms, even down to the layers of magma, and the Earth's core. Then place the south stone at the south point of your circle as you envision above and below working together in complete harmony, nourishing a strong and healthy planet.

9. Refer to the compass to establish the east–west axis of your circle. Pick the stone that will mark the west point of your circle and use your eyes to figure out the point along the western axis that is equidistant from the north and south points.

     Hold the west stone in your hand and call on it to represent the forces of transformation and change. This direction represents all the ideas or beings that are not useful for the health of the whole, and that need to be transformed or recycled.

10. Hold the east stone in your hand and allow it to represent all the potential new beings that may arise here in the future. Say a prayer for a future that will nourish the Earth and strengthen its communities as you place the eastern stone onto the ground.

11. Use more stones or your other materials to line the north–south and east–west axes of the mandala. If you like, you can add decorations to further enhance your mandala by marking the circumference of the circle, the ordinal points (NW, NE, SW, and SE), and the like.

12. When you are done drawing the mandala, spend a few moments inviting all the directions to work together in harmony. Give thanks to the land and all of the beings who participate in this harmony.

Give thanks also to those who have helped you create this template for healing.

13. Begin to withdraw your awareness from your surroundings and focus on your own body's boundaries. As you complete your meditation, check in with the land to see if things feel complete. Say good-bye and walk away.

Rebirth

Nine months after building the stone circle—another gestation—I was ready to move away from the Hudson Valley to Vermont. Before I made the decision to leave, however, I wanted to be certain that I had fulfilled my vow to the river. Had I done what I had promised to help Moheakantuk heal?

These things are notoriously hard to measure. I have heard of land healers who look at before-and-after statistics of crime rates and high school graduation rates and such, to evaluate whether a region has changed in response to healing work. Others turn to farmers, whose exacting records of yields and losses can also provide a good picture of an area's overall health. In theory, I could look at fish-kill statistics or lists of accidents and problems at the power plant.

However, in my acupuncture practice I have learned that while quantifiable changes are powerfully persuasive, they are not usually the first sign of healing to manifest. Instead, something very subjective and entirely unmeasurable usually shows up first: a better night's sleep, less pain, feelings of hope. So I ask my clients how they feel before I ask about their lab results and scans. If I wanted to know how Moheakantuk was feeling, perhaps I could just ask it. So that's what I did.

Sitting in meditation, I called to the river. "Moheakantuk, how are you?" I replayed the image from my original vision, now nearly two years old—those burning forks of lightning from Indian Point searing the river. I recalled the image of myself at the water's edge making a vow to help the river heal; then I envisioned the building of the stone circle in the grand thunderstorm. Then I sat in silence and waited.

In my mind's eye, I saw an image of my spine, which twisted and undulated like a living being. I understood that it was a river of independent consciousness both within me and somehow outside of me—a connection to something larger. Then I saw Moheakantuk—a separate being—yet also in ceaseless motion, turning and rushing through canyons of limestone and granite. Before my eyes the two rivers overlapped and wrapped themselves together. They moved apart, then came together again.

My first thought was that they were two snakes dancing—like the caduceus symbol that represents a healer. Then I saw that the two rivers had woven themselves into a spiral, the primal spiral of a DNA molecule. Recognition jolted through me. *Of course: the river and I are a single being*—braided together from separate strands, it is true, but joined at our very core as life-forms on this planet. Together, and only together, we can constitute a new life.

In this time of Great Turning, our species is racing to create the conditions for something magical to happen; we are seeking to unite with the beings of Earth in a way that allows a spark of new life to take hold among us. Imagine how much will change when we recognize this fundamental truth and begin to act from the certainty of it. When we begin to support the laws and institutions and governments that nourish the Earth and all the beings who live on it. When we replicate the beauty and interdependence and harmony that are still, for now, able to model divinity for us. Then, when we can conceive and nourish this new way of living with all of our relatives—only then will we become parents of a livable future.

Notes

CHAPTER 1. THE DRAGON'S BREATH

1. Carmer, *The Hudson,* 12.
2. Seaby and Henderson, *Entrainment, Impingement and Thermal Impacts.*
3. Stanne, *The Hudson: An Illustrated Guide to the Living River,* 9.

CHAPTER 2. THE PULSE OF THE LAND

1. Cary Institute, "Historic Pollution in the Hudson River," caryinstitute.org.
2. IPSEC, "Indian Point Timeline," http://www.ipsecinfo.org/1952.htm.
3. Halbfinger, "New York Denies Indian Point a Water Permit."

CHAPTER 6. THE EXTRAORDINARY CHANNELS

1. Low, *The Secondary Vessels of Acupuncture,* 146.
2. Seaby and Henderson, *Entrainment, Impingement and Thermal Impacts,* 25.

CHAPTER 7. DIVIDED WATERS

1. McBeth, *The Crystal Journey.*
2. Graves, *Needles of Stone.*
3. Ibid., chapter 4.

CHAPTER 8. THUNDER MOUNTAIN

1. Carmer, *The Hudson*, 107.
2. Irving, *Selections from Washington Irving*, ed. Isaac Thomas, 239–40.
3. Ibid, 240.
4. Ellis, Wiseman, and Boss, *Grasping the Wind*, 30–31.

CHAPTER 10. THE FURIES

1. Vastag, Maese, and Fahrenthold. "U.S. Urges Americans within 50 Miles of Japanese Nuclear Plant to Evacuate; NRC Chief Outlines Dangerous Situation."
2. Sheppard, "Do You Live in a Nuclear Danger Zone?"
3. Applebome, "Fukushima, Indian Point and Fantasy."

CHAPTER 11. PILGRIMAGE

1. Ehrlich, *Questions of Heaven*, 15.
2. Hinton, *Hunger Mountain*, 56.
3. Ehrlich, *Questions of Heaven*, 15.

CHAPTER 16. THE GREAT TURNING

1. Naess and Sessions, "Deep Ecology Platform."
2. Berry, *The Great Work*, 3.
3. Macy, www.joannamacy.net/
4. Berry, *The Great Work*, 20.
5. Roszak, *The Voice of the Earth*, 308.
6. Chetwynd, *Dictionary of Symbols*, 165.

CHAPTER 17. HEALING/RECONCEIVED

1. Vaughan-Lee, *Spiritual Ecology*, ii.
2. Berry, *The Dream of the Earth*, 207–8.
3. Lewis, *Till We Have Faces*, 294.

Bibliography

Applebome, Peter. "Fukushima, Indian Point and Fantasy." *New York Times,* March 20, 2011.

Berry, Thomas. *The Dream of the Earth.* San Francisco: Sierra Club Books, 1988.

——. *The Great Work: Our Way into the Future.* New York: Bell Tower, 1999.

Campbell, Joseph. *The Hero with a Thousand Faces.* Princeton, N.J.: Princeton University Press, 1949.

Carmer, Carl. *The Hudson.* New York: Fordham University Press, 1989.

Cary Institute of Ecosystem Studies. *The Changing Hudson Project.* http://www.caryinstitute.org/educators/teaching-materials/changing-hudson-project.

Chetwynd, Tom. *Dictionary of Symbols.* London: Aquarian Press, 1993.

Deadman, Peter, and Mazin Al-Khafaji, with Kevin Baker. *A Manual of Acupuncture.* Hove, UK: Journal of Chinese Medicine Publications, 2001.

Dunwell, Frances F. *The Hudson River Highlands.* New York: Columbia University Press, 1991.

Ehrlich, Gretel. *Questions of Heaven.* Boston: Beacon Press, 1998.

Ellis, Andrew, Nigel Wiseman, and Ken Boss. *Grasping the Wind: An Exploration into the Meaning of Chinese Acupuncture Point Names.* Brookline, Mass.: Paradigm, 1989.

Graves, Tom. *Needles of Stone.* London: HarperCollins, 1980. Downloaded from http://www.isleofavalon.co.uk/GlastonburyArchive/ (Accessed November 25, 2014).

Halbfinger, David M. "New York Denies Indian Point a Water Permit." *New York Times,* April 3, 2010.

Halifax, Joan. *The Fruitful Darkness: Reconnecting with the Body of the Earth.* New York: HarperCollins, 1993.

Hinton, David. *Hunger Mountain: A Field Guide to Mind and Landscape.* Boston: Shambhala Publications, 2012.

IPSEC. "Indian Point Timeline." http://www.ipsecinfo.org/1952.htm (Accessed November 25, 2014).

Irving, Washington. *Selections from Washington Irving.* Edited by Isaac Thomas. Boston: Leach, Shewell, & Sanborn, 1894.

Kalweit, Holger. *Shamans, Healers, and Medicine Men.* Boston: Shambhala Publications, 1992.

Kaptchuk, Ted J. *The Web That Has No Weaver: Understanding Chinese Medicine.* New York: Congdon & Weed, 1983.

Lewis, C. S. *Till We Have Faces: A Myth Retold.* San Diego: Harcourt Brace, 1984.

Low, Royston. *The Secondary Vessels of Acupuncture.* Wellingborough, UK: Thorsons Publishers, 1983.

Macy, Joanna. www.joannamacy.net. (Accessed December 1, 2014).

McBeth, Ivan. *The Crystal Journey: Apprenticed to the Earth.* Bloomington, Ind.: Xlibris, 2005.

Naess, Arne, and George Sessions. "The Deep Ecology Platform." 1984. http://www.deepecology.org/platform.htm (Accessed November 25, 2014).

Narby, Jeremy. *The Cosmic Serpent: DNA and the Origins of Knowledge.* New York: Jeremy P. Tarcher/Putnam, 1998.

Plotkin, Bill. *Nature and the Human Soul.* Novato, Calif.: New World Library, 2008.

Roszak, Theodore. *The Voice of the Earth.* New York: Simon & Schuster, 1992.

Seaby, Richard M. H., and Peter A. Henderson. *Entrainment, Impingement and Thermal Impacts at Indian Point Nuclear Power Station.* Lymington, UK: Pisces Conservation, 2007.

Sheppard, Kate. "Do You Live in a Nuclear Danger Zone?" *Mother Jones,* March 22, 2011.

Stanne, Stephen P. *The Hudson: An Illustrated Guide to the Living River.* New Brunswick, N.J.: Rutgers University Press, 1996.

Vastag, Brian, Rick Maese, and David A. Fahrenthold. "U.S. Urges Americans within 50 Miles of Japanese Nuclear Plant to Evacuate; NRC Chief Outlines Dangerous Situation." *Wall Street Journal,* March 16, 2011.

Vaughan-Lee, Llewellyn. *Spiritual Ecology: The Cry of the Earth.* Point Reyes, Calif.: Golden Sufi Center, 2013.

Index

Page numbers in *italics* indicate photographs and illustrations.

of fawn, 124

symbols of, during project, 175–76

blackout. *See* Northeast blackout of
2003

Buchanan, town of, 101–2

Building a Stone Mandala to Balance
Earth Energies (exercise), 181–83

bundles, Native American, 134–35, 145

Capuchin monastery, Garrison, NY
circle of trees, 112–13
as Heart Protector point, 126
visit with Ivan and Lucie, 126–27
visit with James and Laura, 111–13

chess, symbolism of, 166–67

church bells, 127

Classic of Difficulties, 70

Cole, Thomas, 13

Conception Vessel, 62–65, *63, 64,
65,* 67–68, 77, 157, 177. *See also*
Hudson River Valley

Connecting with a Larger Landscape
and Finding its Pulse Points
(exercise), 114–16

Consolidated Edison, 13, 69

Council of All Beings, 163–64

Creating a Relationship with a Tree
(exercise), 59–60

Croton River, 29–30

Crystal Journey, The (McBeth), 73

crystals
digging for quartz, 73–74
dreams following use, 127
placed at Capuchin monastery,
Garrison, NY, 126–27
placed on Dunderberg Mountain,
122–23, 145

Tintagel, 122, 127

Deep Ecology, 163

depression experienced during project,
107–10

Devil's Horse Race, 17, 84–85

DNA
carving on tree, 91
at conception, 176–77
metaphor for Hudson River, 185
return to human roots, 178

Doodletown Bight, 36

dowsing by Patrick MacManaway
of author's yard, 147
of Dunderberg, from a distance, 175
and Earth acupuncture, 172–73

dragon's breath, 12

Dream of the Earth, The (Berry), 163

dreams
after planting crystals, 127
of healing Lyme disease, 165–66

Dr. Susan, 167–68

Druidic geomancy, 118–27

Dunderberg Mountain
Devil's Horse Race, 84–85
hiking with Ivan and Lucie, 121–25
hiking with Ivan, James, and Patrick,
141–46
hiking with James, 56–58, 89–95,
141–46
hiking with Sarah and Jerry, 174–75
and Hudson River, *81,* 81–82, *86, 87*
as Lung 7 point (Lie Que), 85–88,
86, 87
prayers to, 83
satellite view of, *81, 87*
spirit of, 84–85